Education in the Age of Globalisation

EDUCATION IN THE AGE OF GLOBALISATION

Edited by

Dr. Sudhansu Sekhar Mishra

Dr. Rajan Kumar Sahoo

Dr. (Mrs.) Tilottama Senapati

Reference Press

New Delhi

Education in the Age of Globalisation

ISBN: 978-81-8405-056-1

Rs.500/-

First Indian Imprint 2009

Published by:
Reference Press
4831/24, Ansari Road,
Darya Ganj,
New Delhi-110 002.
INDIA
Phones: 23260807, 41563444
Fax: 41563334
E-mail: info@essessreference.com
www.essessreference.com

Printed and bound in India at Salasar Imaging Systems.

Contents

Preface

Globalisation is a process of integration of the national economy with the world economy as a result of which national market will be linked with international market and the restrictions will be progressively abolished. Globalisation of education refers to the operation of educational services on a world wide scale. It is internationalization which refers to the co-operation between nations in order to develop standards of educational services. After the introduction of Economic Reform by India in 1991, replacement of General Agreement on Trade and Tariff (GATT) by World Trade Organisation (WTO) in 1995 and signing of General Agreement on Trade in Services (GATS) in 1996, the process gained momentum. The signing of GATS by WTO member countries has made education a tradable commodity determined by the market forces i.e. demand and supply. Education being one of the 12 classified sectors, covering 161 services works with a specified legal framework. In this changing scenario, education has been divided into 5 classifications i.e. Primary Education, Secondary Education, Higher Education (including post secondary, technical and vocational education services), Adult Education, and other Education (testing and certification). There are four modes of delivery of education services like cross border supply (distance mode), consumption abroad (students studying abroad), commercial Presence (Campus abroad) and presence of Natural Persons (Faculty teaching abroad).

The crux of globalisation in education sector is that the teaching learning is no longer for 'building nation' but a business for 'profit making'. Many educational institutions formed during post independence era like IITS are adopting U.S. Massachusetts Institute of Technology Model, IIMS created adopting Harvard Business School Model and IGNOU carved out of U.K. experience are going to be influenced by globalisation. How the Indian institutions are going to carry out their vision and mission in future in the light of the entry of Global players in the educational service sector and what type of changes have emerged and what sort of challenges they pose is the concern of all the stake holders of education.

The present work is the outcome of the research work of many researchers, senior faculty members and educationists. The researchers have studied the emerging trends of education, new challenges they pose and the possible crisis they apprehend collecting data both from primary and secondary sources. It is certain that, the valuable contributions, views and suggestions of the researchers will be of immense help to the future researchers, policy makers, administrators, social thinkers and educationists in solving the problems of this sector and to introduce policy measures for the educational development in general and higher education in particular of the state and the country.

Acknowledgements

We, the editors of the volume owe our deepest sense of gratitude and indebtedness to University Grants Commission, (Eastern Regional Office) LB-8, Sector III, Salt Lake, Kolkata –700098, for the financial support to organize a National Level Conference, otherwise it would have been impossible.

We will fail in our duty, if we do not acknowledge our indebtedness to Dr. V.B.Shastri, Professor and former Principal, Radhanath Institute of Advanced Studies in Education, Cuttack who despite of his busy schedule has come to inaugurate the U.G.C. Sponsored National Level Conference on 28th January 2007, in the college premises, 90kms away from his residence located at Bhubaneswar and inspired the delegates addressing on "The Emerging Trends in Education in the age of Globalization."

Mr Manoj Kumar Mohapatra a noted writer and general Manager (Human Resource) IMFA Group of Industries, Bhubaneswar needs a special mention as he has discussed on the process of globalisation which is going on in the country and its possible problems and prospects on different sectors, especially education.

No words are adequate to express our thankfulness to Dr. R.P.Das, Professor and Dean

Faculty of Management Studies, Dr Rabishankar Sukla University, Raipur, Chhattishgarh, Dr (Mrs) Bharati Mohapatra, former Principal, Nalini Devi Women's College, of Teacher Education, Bhubaneswar, Captain Dr Gouranga Charan Sahoo, Head Department of Commerce, Kendrapara Autonomous College, Kendrapara (Orissa) and Dr Sudhansu Sekhar Mohapatra, Reader in Commerce, Sikkim Government College, Ganktok who have successfully conducted the technical session of the conference, delivered keynote address and enlightened the delegates, students and staff of the college acting as Chairperson, Keynote speaker and Resource persons respectively.

We are deeply indebted to the invited guests, delegates, paper writers, media persons, local elites and educationists present who despite of their own personal inconveniences came forward with all enthusiasm and devoted quite a lot of their precious time to make the conference a grand success, otherwise the volume could have been impossible.

We are grateful to Principal, Prof Jogesh Chandra Pati, staff and students of U.N.S. Mahavidyalaya, Khairabad, Mugpal, Jajpur (Orissa), without their co-operation, organization of conference and publication of conference volume could not have been imagined.

It is a great pleasure to acknowledge the inestimable help received from Prof. Rabindranath Samal, Administrative Bursar, Prof. Ramachandra Sahoo, Reader in History, Dr. (Mrs.) Susmita Mishra, Reader in History, Dr. Dhruba Charan Nayak, Lecturer in Oriya, Prof. Nrusingha Charan Tripathy, Lecturer in History, Prof. Hariballav Dash, Lecturer in Education, Miss Muktilata Das, Lecturer in Sanskrit,

Dr Braja Kishore Nayak, Lecturer in Oriya, Prof. Dillip Kumar Chakra, Lecturer in English, Prof. Sidhartha Shankar Rath, Lecturer in History, Prof. Ramesh Chandra Bhoi, Lecturer in Education of U.N.S. Mahavidyalaya, in providing instinct co-operation and ungrudging help.

To name a few, we must thank Sri Surendra Kumar Tripathy, Head Clerk, Janardan Sahoo, Accountant, Rajkishore Kar, Sr. Clerk, Biswanath Panda, Cashier, Baban Charan Dash, Accounts Clerk, Shantilata Sahu, Demonstrator Physics, Bijoy Kumar Satapathy, Demonstrator Chemistry, Manoj Kumar Mohapatra, Demonstrator, Zoology, Rabindra Kumar Khuntia, Basanta Kumar Mishra, Ananta Charan Panda, Narayan Malik, and Kulamani Malik employees of this institute for their untiring help and the people of Rasulpur block, Jajpur (Orissa) for their silent support and co-operation.

Ranjan Kumar Dalai of Radhanath I.A.S.E., Cuttack deserves special mention as he has neatly computerized the entire work.

At last we extend our thanks to M/s Reference Press, New Delhi, for releasing this work within the record time

Editors

1

Emerging Trends in Education in the Age of Globalisation

Prof. (Dr.) V.B. Shastri
Former Principal, Radhanath I.A.S.E.,
Cuttack – 753002.

INTRODUCTION

Globalisation is a steadily evolving and expanding concept. Narrow nationalism is dangerous; but galloping globalisation is a glowing ball of fire which may totally efface national cultures and idealities. National interests and global concerns need to be balanced. We should not be swayed away by emotional slogans. The stakes are seriously high and they should be thoroughly analysed by economists, sociologists, educationists, defence analysts and policy planners. A lot of discussion regarding the pros and cons of globalisation needs to precede a final decision.

Globalisation is not a totally good remedy to the divided world order; nor is it an unmitigated evil. The global future is critical and crucial. It concerns all. But national interests can never be forgotten in the name of globalisation. We have to strike a balance. The global and local must merge to give rise to a finely tuned 'glocal' approach.

Is globalisation really global? Or is it the forceful lobby of Euro-American developed nations? We have the UNO; but its advice is ignored by bullying super powers. We may have 'globalisation of education' which may ultimately degenerate into backdoor intellectual colonialism of the developed nations. Before plunging it, globalisation a thread bare national debate should precede. Ultimately, we may apt for 'limited' or ' conditional' globalisation' safeguarding our culture and sovereignty.

MEANING OF OPERATIONAL TERMS

— Emerging means 'becoming gradually visible' and ' facts become known.'

— 'Trends' denote ' a general direction in which something is developing or changing'.

— 'Education' is ' the process of teaching and learning and also includes ' the process of training'

— 'Age' denotes ' a distinct period of time'

— 'Globalisation means,

1. ' operate world –wide'.
2. Removal of barriers to free trade and the close integration of national economy. (Goseph Stigler, Nobel Laureate in Economics –2002, in 'Globalisation and in its Discontent Penguin, ix.
3. Integration of economies and societies through cross –country flow of information, ideas, technology, goods, services, capital, finance, and people. C. Rangarajan, Ex-

Governor of Reserved Bank of India in 'Indian Economy Since Independence, New Delhi, Frederic foundation, 2003 p. 725.)

Britannica Ready Reference Encyclopaedia (2005) defines 'globalisation' as: "Process by which the experience of every day, life market by the diffusion of commodities and ideas, is becoming standardized around the world. Factors that have contributed to globalization include increasingly sophisticated communications and transportation technologies and services, mass migration and the movement of the people, a level of economic activity that has outgrown national markets through industrial combinations and commercial groupings that cross national frontiers, and international agreements that reduce the cost of doing business in foreign countries. Globalization offers huge potential to companies and nations that has been complicated by widely differing expectations, standards of living, cultures and values, and legal systems as well as unexpected global cause-and –effect linkages". (Page 169, Vol.4)

DEVELOPMENTS AUGMENTING GLOBALIZATION OF EDUCATION

The General Agreement on Tariffs and Trade was established on Ist January, 1948 to regulate and bring order to international trade after the Second World War. In 1995, it was replaced by the World Trade Organisation. It is an international body which purports to promote free trade by persuading countries to abolish import tariffs and other barriers. It indirectly promotes the culture of globalisation. It covers trade in commodities and services such as advertising, banking, communication, intellectual property rights etc.

Its address is: World Trade Organisation Centre William Rappard, 154 Rue de Lausanee CH-1211 P.O. Geneva –21, Switzerland. Its Website is: *http:// wwww.wto*. Org. Its present Director General is Mr. Pascal Lamy of France.

GATS AND TRADE IN SERVICES

International trade was confined to trade in goods. Trades in services started as an additional component of international trade. It was small, insignificant and was in the marginalia. It was not taken seriously. However, in the last decade of the 20th century it emerged as a major business venture. The member states of the World Trade Organisation had agreed to sign General Agreement on Trade in Services (GATS) 2006 to promote progressive liberalization; non-discrimination; free, fair, and transparent market conditions to secure commercial transactions in the service sector.

GATS & EDUCATION

Education is a service. Quality education is universally praised and prized. Quality education provides the passport to the knowledge society. Countries with high quality educational systems had magnetic attraction. They are at the supplying end.

The demand for quality education emerges from developing countries that need to train skilled manpower and countries with a weak higher education system. Easy and speedy communication facilitates it. The prestige-tag attached to foreign qualifications is another driving force.

ACADEMIC AREAS WITH POTENTIAL GROWTH

Education is a mosaic of many disciplines. All subjects do not have equal global attraction. Some specialization are likely to attract the maximum number of scholars in view of the emerging economy of the first three decades of the 21st century upto 2030. They are:

i. Management and Commerce.
ii. Information and Communication Technology.
iii. Health Science with focus on the health of the aged people.

CONDITIONS THAT PROMOTE EDUCATIONAL GLOBALIZATION

People go to a foreign country to gain quality education. But, in the sphere of quality education there are many countries competing with each other. It is concluded on the basis of a close study that foreign students choice of a country for further study depends upon the following factors:

i. Cost of studying abroad.
ii. The policies of the country where quality education is available.
iii. Nearness to one's own country.

The combined computed cost of tuition fees plus living expenses were the highest in U.S.A. and the lowest in New Zealand in 2001. Therefore, many scholars are opting to go to New Zealand and other comparatively lower-cost countries like Australia and Canada.

ADVANTAGES AND DISADVANTAGES OF GLOBALIZATION OF EDUCATION

Globalisation of Education has its advantages and disadvantages.

Advantages

- Free flow of Capital from other countries.
- Free flow of best pedagogical practices.
- Increased use of ICT.
- Spread of educational facilities throughout the world.
- Balanced development of world education.
- Increased flow of students and teachers to and from the countries.
- National education and culture through cross fertilization of ideas.
- High quality education at affordable prices.
- Transfer of educational ideas and skills.
- Increased educational exchanges.
- Better income and higher status.
- Human Development across the world.
- A better international knowledge skills.

Disadvantages

- National educational system gets neglected and undernourished.
- Exploits the local teaching community by demeaning its prestige.
- Loss of jobs in the educational field for intellectuals of the native country.
- Decreasing enrolment in native educational institutions.
- Decline in the income of the academician of the country.
- Intellectual colonialism imposed through knowledge.
- Leads to educational and cultural imperialism.
- Neglect of local culture and folkloristics.
- Neglect of non economic culture –specific subjects.
- There would be more money in the pockets of more people but lesser culture and refinement.

Fig. 1. Globalisation of Education

IMPLICATIONS FOR INDIAN EDUCATION

- The forecast of growth in overseas students of British Council portrays a hopeful picture. India occupies the third position, but is far behind China.
- Foreign students flocking to Indian Universities and Colleges are mostly from countries of East Asia, Middle East, and the neighbouring countries

viz., China, North Korea, South Korea, Jordan, Kuwait, Oman, Malaysia, Indonesia, Bangladesh, Sri Lanka and Nepal.

- Students of African origin are mainly from the countries of Sudan, Ethiopia, Kenya and Tanzania.
- It is disturbing to note that the number of foreign students had drastically decreased during the period 1990-91 to 2000 –01.
- 61,812 Indian students had gone abroad and only 6,896 foreign students had come to India for study in 2000-01. These figures clearly reveal the quality of Indian institutions of higher education. It is very low.
- From India, the flow of students in 2002-03 to U.S. A was 74,603, to the United Kingdom approximately 9000 and Germany 3,0303.

INDIAN EDUCATION AND GLOBALISATION: GROWTH TRENDS

A study of the British Council has provided the forecast of growth in overseas students for different countries. Table No. 1 provides these figures.

Table 1. Forecast in Growth of Overseas Students

Sl.No	*Country*	*2010*	*2020*	*Remarks*
1.	China	59,900	1,44,900	Including Hon Kong
2.	Greece	30,900	34,800	
3.	India	16,500	29,800	
4.	Malaysia	14,500	28,400	
5.	Ireland	14,800	17,900	
6.	U.S.A	14,300	16,000	
7.	Germany	14,400	15,800	
8.	France	13,000	14,700	
9.	Pakistan	4,800	11,100	

The projections are optimistic; but time alone can testify whether these projections would become realities or not.

INITIATIVES TO ATTRACT FOREIGN STUDENTS TO INDIA

i. The Government of India has launched a scheme called DASA (Direct Administration of Students Abroad). It has reserved seats in elite educational institutions like IITs, IIMs, NITs for NRIs and persons of Indian origin.

ii. The UGC has initiated a programme known as PIHEAD – Promotion of Indian Higher Education Abroad. Though PIHEAD Indian Educational Fairs are held in foreign countries; promotional advertising literature and software like brochures, booklets, C.Ds and Websites are widely distributed. Short-term non-degree programmes are launched. Programmes are held to increase the awareness relating to Indian Universities and Colleges of excellence. EdCil (Educational Consultants of India Limited) has been assigned the responsibility of marketing Indian education aboard.

iii. India hopes to have a big share in the educational market of Asian and African countries.

CONCLUSION

It is the quality which holds the key to become a major global player in the field of education. The islands of educational excellence like IITs, IIITS, IIMs NIFT, NID are sure to harvest a good crop. But, out of the 350 Universities in India even twenty Universities do not have the quality parameters to attract foreign students. The danger bells are already ringing. By May,

2006, 150 foreign universities had already set their shops in India with an enrolment of 8000 students. It is a dangerous emerging trend with the potential of completely over shadowing the colleges and Universities of India. If the Indian academicians do not take timely action for quality assurance, then globalisation would bring the darkest clouds to the Indian educational scene. It is time to rise and face the dangers of the gathering storm of globalisation of education. Improve the quality of education or commit socio- cultural and intellectual suicide. Let us be reminded of the clarion call of Swami Vivekananda - "Uttishta, Jagrath, Barannibodhata".

REFERENCES

1. Oxford University Press, "*Compact Oxford Dictionary Thesaurus and Word power Guide*" 2005 OUP, New Delhi.
2. *Britannica Ready Reference Encyclopaedia*, 2005
3. *Monorama Year Book*, 2007.
4. Rao, K. Sudha and Singh K. Mithilesh, "*University Education in India: Challenges Ahead*" in University News Vol. 45 No.2, p-6.
5. British Council, "*Forecast Growth in Overseas Students.*
6. Ahmed, Nighat, "*Global Student Mobility: Opportunities and Challenges*" University News, Vol 42, No.5, Dec 13-19, 2004, p- 9,
7. Ibid. P. 10
8. Ahmed, Nighat, " *Cross Border Marketing of Higher Education*" University News, Vol. 43 No.9, Feb – March, 2005, p-6.
9. K.B. Power, Veena Bhalla and Shikha Tiwari. "*International Student Mobility*", University News, Vol.43, No.5, Jan-Feb. 2005, p - 3.
10. Shastry, V.B., " *Challenges of Globalization to Education and Quality Imperatives*" in Souvenir of the National Seminar 18-19th Feb 2006 of College of Teacher Education, Rourkela, Keynote Address, pp. - 1 to 4.

2

Emerging Trends in Higher Education in the Global Era

Sri Bhagabata Behera
Department of Commerce,
Bhadrak Autonomous College,
Bhadrak, Balasore.

This paper presents an analytical account of some of the prominent emerging trends in higher education in the global era. It describes the changing pattern of higher education i.e. traditional (conventional) to new /market oriented pattern under the impact of globalisation.

The importance of education is recognized in every society. Education and knowledge are viewed as great wealth in themselves. Education is also viewed as an instrument of personal development, expansion of intellectual horizons of individuals and an instrument of social engineering. It also recognized as a powerful instrument for the development of human potentialities and empowering people to have better quality of life.

Recognizing the importance of education, in the traditional societies, the state was assigned a major role in spreading education and dissemination of knowledge. State led education was viewed as an instrument of 'public good' and as a mechanism for promoting 'equity, 'democracy' and 'social justice'. Education including the higher education was 'highly subsidized and the system of education was supported by state funding.

But since 1990s, there has been a paradigm shift in the pattern of education in India. After the economic liberalization that started in the nineties paved the way for the globalisation of educational services in India under the General Agreement in Trade & Services (GATS). As per the norms of the agreement, the state has opened the higher education sector for private participation. Market more particularly private sector holds the key of the educational sector. Correspondingly a reduced role of the state in education, more explicitly higher education is promoted. It is argued that the role of state should be confined to the formulation of a coherent policy framework.

The creeping of a market philosophy into higher education, which is more in gained in the American psyche has come as something of cultural shock to Indian People. Due to liberalization, there is a drastic cut of public expenditure on higher education and promotion of market in the educational sector. Infact government polices in the liberal era have set the tone for drastic reforms in higher education. Along with this, there is a public apathy towards higher education. There is also a change of public attitude towards higher education and the attitude is directed towards private higher education and for profit oriented higher institutions of higher education, in particular. The 'public' and 'merit' good nature of higher education is being increasingly discounted. Private higher education is projected as an efficient system that can improve access and quality as well as equity.

Under the impact of globalisation, government have either explicitly encourage higher education institutions to adopt market relevant policies, or implicitly formulated policies that contribute to rapid privatization of higher education. Such policies include: withdrawal of government grants and funds, introduction of marketable courses' of study which can be 'sold to the students', appointment of industrialists as heads or chairmen of the governing bodies of higher education institutions.

The march towards marketisation of higher education is taking place through a variety of measures: financial privatization of public universities, transfer of ownership of public institutions and establishment of private institutions. Private institutions with government support, self-financing and all focusing on short term market considerations and immediate market relevance. The emerging private institutions also consist more of institutions without government recognition. Universities also began to transfer themselves into entrepreneurial universities and autonomy from the government has also become a buzzword. The purpose of universities, their ownership, sources of revenue, norms of management and the role of the government in university and college development has been changing very fast. The changes are not confined to newly established universities or institutions, but even the universities established several decades ago, are affected by the changes and there is a steady march from public ness to high private ness in higher education.

The emerging scenario of higher education may

be depicted in the following tables.

Table 1. Emerging Trends in Planning, Policy and Financing of Higher Education

Conventional/ Traditional Model	*Emerging Model*
Welfare Approach	Market Approach
Public Higher Education	Mixed/Private Higher Education
Public Financing	Private Financing
Private Govt. recognized institutions	Private Institutions requiring no government recognition
Private-Philanthropic & educational consideration.	Private–commercial motives private motives.
No fees	Introduction of fees
Low level of fees	High level of fees.
No student loan	Introduction of student loan.
Scholarly/academic disciplines of study	Self- financing /commercial viable/ profitable disciplines of study.
Emphasis on formal/fulltime education	Open/ Distance/ Part-time Education
Selection of Criteria of Heads-	Selection of criteria heads of
Academic background	-Expertise in financial/ money management and in resource generation.

Source : Tilak (1999)

Table 2. Comparative Trends in Higher Education:

Area of concern	*Traditional Model*	*Market Oriented Model*
Motivation	Service	Profit
Main concern	Knowledge	Skill
Area of interest	Generic	Specific
Duration of interest	Long term	Short term

Team effort	Rarely/ Occasionally	Always
Research / Publication	Public good	Private good/ confidential
Time schedule	Flexible	Rigid

Table 3. Comparative Dimensions in Traditional and Global / Market Education

Dimension	*Traditional Model*	*Market Oriented Model*
Mission/ Purpose	Serve as public mission determined by the state	Mission serves private interest of students, clients and owners.
Ownership	Public	Mixed/Private later Pvt. for profit.
Source of finance/ revenue	Public/Tax payer	Mainly private but some public assistance.
Control	State/Government	High degree of Autonomy/limited state control (Almost no state control)
Norms of Management	Academic norms / shared governance	Limited acceptance to academic norms, high management control. (Operated like business management).

Source: John stone (1999)

The emerging trends of privatization of higher education may be analysed in the following manner:

First, 'an extreme version ' of privatization implying total privatization of higher education, colleges and universities being managed and founded by the private sector, with little government intervention.

Second, there is 'strong' degree of privatization which means recovery of full costs of public higher education from the users.

Third, there is a moderate form of privatization implying public provision of higher education but with reasonable level of financing from non-government sources.

In short, the emerging higher education system may be summarized as transformation of academic institutions into "entrepreneurial universities" and "commercial institutions", the single most important objectives of which seems to be mobilization of more and more resources and creation of "higher education bazar" all over the India.

CONCLUDING OBSERVATION

The emerging trends in higher education is posing a serious threat to our conventional pattern of higher education and learning in terms of access, quality and equity. In fact the process of globalisation has created a gap between the knowledge operating in the global plane and knowledge the Indian society possesses. Let us understand that the globalisation will only promote knowledge relating to scientific and technological field to suit the needs of the global market. It is not going to promote traditional knowledge based on a ethics and morality. Therefore, the need of hour is to understand the changing needs and realities of the global world and prepare ourselves to face the challenge. In view of this there is a urgent need to revamp our educational curriculum to fit the changing needs of the world. In the end we may say that the intelligentia, academician, policy makers and the civil society has a big role to play to sensitise the people and update and upgrade our educational system to suit the structural and functional needs of the world.

REFERENCES

1. Arrow, K. J. 1993): *'Excellence and Equity in Higher Education'*, Education Economics 1 (1): 5-12.
2. Bok, D. (2003): *Universities in the Market Place: the Commercialization of Higher Education*, Princeton University Press, Princeton.
3. Johnson, G.E. (1984): *'Subsidies for Higher Education'*, Journal of Labour Economics 2 (3): 303-18.
4. John Stone, B. (1999): *'Privatisation in and of Higher Education in US'*, Buffalo Education, PP 1-3.
5. Mishra, R.C. (1996): *'The Welfare of Nation'* in R Boyer and D Drache (eds), *States against Markets: The Limits of Globalization*, Roult ledge, London, pp 316-33.
6. Tilak J.B.G. (1991): ' *Privatisation of Higher Education Prospective*, Quarterly Review of Education (UNESCO), 21 (2): PP 227-39.
7. ____ (1999): *Emerging Trends and Evolving Public Policies on Privatisation of Higher Education in India'* in P.G. Altoach (ed). Private Promethus: Private Higher Education and Development in the 21st Century, Green wood Publishing, West port, pp. 113-35.
8. UNDP (2004): *Human Development Report*, Oxford, New Delhi.

3

Education in the Era of Globalisation: Some Emerging Trends

Dr Sangram Kumar Mohapatra
HOD, Economics, Simulia College,
Markona, Balasore, (Orissa)

BACKDROP

After independence in the era of planned economic development in India, Indian education began to grow very rapidly. Today India's progress in all fronts, in world's largest network is contributed by education. India has one of the largest pools of manpower in science and technology. The institutions in India in this regard like IITs, IIMs, AIIMS, IISE, JNU, DU are the better universities and are considered as the better even in the world. It is also quite instrumental that within the selected few countries of the world India's rank no doubt is higher sometimes that it has the capability to develop super computer, IT advancement, fast breeder reactor's satellites and satellite launch vehicles etc. Industrialization and agricultural development have reached far beyond the expectations through the length and breadth and started to share with international competition world over in terms of quality and efficiency.

ESSENCE OF EDUCATION IN GLOBALISATION PERSPECTIVES

With the advent of time, the challenges of life have multiplied. The process of globalisation has brought people closer to one another. It removes the barriers to free trade. It makes closer integration of national economies. In economic sense, globalisation refers to the integration of different economies of the world through trades, investment and migration of the people. It means integration of the people in the economies and societies through cross-country, flow of information, ideas, technology, goods and services capital and finance and people. Connectivity is the essence of globalisation. Hence, it can be concluded that more free trade means more welfare of the people. The revolution of the world in IT and ET has rendered education most portable, flexible and viable, non-linear and student–centric. Globalisation in education refers to integrating an international dimension in teaching, learning and service functions of the institutions.

There was a time when the world was big and slow in changing. Today the world is fast changing. The boundaries and the barriers amongst the nation have almost vanished. It is becoming small day by day. It is quick in wearing a new garb. The whole world has shrunk into a small village. The process of globalisation has brought people to one another and as such its spectrum is becoming from wide to wider day by day. The student is no longer a citizen of his own land. He is regarded as a world citizen. So he has to be taught trained and developed from larger perspective of globalisation.

EDUCATION: A RELAY RACE IN PRESENT SCENARIO

The top world competition in the present scenario has become a relay race in the field of education. If someone steps into the track of the 21st Century much would be visualized. The only two alternatives crop up is either participate or perish in the long race of cut-throat competition, but there is no third way out to chalk out solutions for multifarious problems. As the supply of the useful knowledge is infinite and easily coming like a rushing wind from every corner of the world, it happens to be a global village, the demand is only for the excellent and high quality goods. The price of education is determined by the basic laws of economics in terms of demand and supply. As a result of this unique and unprecedented situation, the quality of higher education is coupled with consumer satisfaction at competitive cost.

FEATURES OF HIGHER EDUCATION IN INDIA VIS-À-VIS AMERICA

Inspite of various transformations made and impressive achievements undertaken to develop educational systems, it can not be considered as an unqualified success. India has the highest number of illiterates in the world. The quality of education at primary, secondary, colleges and universities level is not upto mark. It is a matter of grave concern that the benefits of growth and development in science and technology is not at all earmarked. It has not reached to the common mass. The quality of higher education (HE) in the country is deteriorating as a consequence of quantitative expansion. Some private institutions in U.S.A. are providing excellent education without govt. support. Peaceful, academic activities with better learning environment including strict rules and regulations are the features of higher education found in America. The state-run institutions cannot meet its requirements because of paucity of funds. In U.S.A. Cornell University which has been set up more than 130 years ago with a lump sum donation, from Ezra Cornell, a self made man with Govt. support becomes the institution of excellence. In India being an under developed country also Manipal Institutions have been spread and providing quality education.

COMMERCIALIZATION AND PROFIT MAXIMIZATION: THE TWIN GOALS OF PRIVATIZATION

Privatisation of higher education (HE) leads to commercialization which brings more profit in comparison to Government counter part and Government managed institutions. The Government colleges and Government institutions located in cities, the benefit goes to urbanites and the student living in the urban areas. The need of the hour is to establish institutions of higher education in rural areas to uplift the rural people from illiteracy and increase the number of literates. More capitation fees and donation from the people will be collected.

The motive behind privatization is not the "Attainment of Education for All". Some professional colleges of Medicine, Engineering, IT and Education by Management Institutions have been established under patronage of politicians who collect huge money as capitation fees to give quality education. Education has become almost a business in the present world irrespective of countries either developed or underdeveloped. Education is not a factory. It is a man making industry. The bright examples are Private Medical and Engineering Colleges. It is a knowledge industry where the industrial manager is a successful top-level bureaucrat. One of the drawbacks of privatization is, it lacks national development.

In India, not more than 4 per cent of its GDP is spent for the purpose of HE. This is below the internationally accepted average of 6 per cent. From the low level only one tenth is spent on HE. Therefore extending HE activities to a large number of people on the one hand and improving its quality on the other would be a cry in the wilderness. Hence the immediate task before the govt. should be to generate more resources for financing education in general and transferring a great deal of resources in favour of HE in particular. So in India funds for HE can be generated mainly from three sources. (a) Govt. either Central or State, (b) from students themselves (c) other sources from philanthropy, industry and sale of publications etc.

HE: A STATE AT UNDOING ACTIVITY

However a cursory look at some data reveals that HE in India has remained in " a state of funding activity" Govt. funding increases from 49.4 percent to 75.9 per cents in 1950-51 to 1986 –87 respectively.(JBG Tilak 2004) Funds from other two sources namely fees and other miscellaneous sources have declined sharply from 36.8 to 12.6 and 13.8 to 11.5 percents respectively in the same above years under discussion . The share of fees during the same period has declined almost three times. On the contrary significant increase can be noticed following an increase of enrollment of the students in India.

QUALITY EDUCATION: THE ULTIMATE GOAL OF ECONOMIC DEVELOPMENT IN INDIA

A country's economic and technological progress depend a great deal on its military and political strength which greatly depend on "Quality Education" to be imparted by Teachers at HE level . So Govt. should come forward to bear its cost otherwise a significant percentage of population would be debarred from HE. The present debate over subsidization of education has become the correct thinking in the cyclic process of advancement in the field of education. As GDP level in India in education scenario especially HE is low and while one fifth of our population is absolutely poor and down trodden and a great majority of Indians are not significantly better, it is very difficult to garner resources for a decent living, the possibility of HE, resources is quite remote.

In the context of present scenario the following things are questionable:

(i) Should the state continue to finance higher education?

(ii) Should students and their parents meet a larger share of cost by way of enhancement of fees and fines?

(iii) Should private sector be asked for to bear a greater share of expenditure on higher education?

These issues should be seriously addressed in the context of prevailing conditions of India. The own method is necessary to develop funds for HE. The model over the globe for financing HE can not be adopted as models for India in this present context.

HIGHER EDUCATION AS NON- MERIT GOOD: THE NEW PERCEPTION OF GOVT

Education as per constitutional provisions is considered as 'public good' also as merit good'. Merit goods because of their over riding importance should be provided even if their members of the society do not demand them. In a free market these goods are under consumed, because of ignorance and externalities. If the provision of education is left to the market then the cost of educating the children will have to be borne by their parents. In this sense higher education, its opportunities from which Indian students would be deprived of is questionable too. The brilliant scholars will be at home. Precious lives will be lost if it is left to the market forces. In this sense, it can be told that the state should either take up the case of supply of merit goods or itself subsidize their availability. Another important aspect and issue of providing HE in India is that the cost is rising day by day. It is a high cost era in which we have entered High Cost education presently relates to fees paid but it is reflected in Govts. allotment of funds for education. Here also a good number of students 'pursuing higher education would find it difficult to pay and continue their education. In this context Indian economy is considered as a 'glass-house economy' having the notion of socio economic ramifications. Govt. for socio-economic conditions transformation should be bountiful in bearing the rising cost of HE to ensure economic equity and social justice.

OBJECTIVES AND METHODOLOGY

In this context this study of the researcher wants to investigate triple objectives of some emerging trends of education in the era of globalisation in general and Higher Education in particular.

(i) Education being a public or a merit good, how far it is successful?

(ii) The discussion of market failure in assuming optimal supply of merit good or public good leads to the increasing number of illiterates in the economy.

(iii) To judge that how far Indian economy has entered into a high cost era and unable to provide higher education from govt. funding agencies.

This study is completely under taken basing upon data collected from secondary information

In early 90's the Govt. of India introduced a number of Economic reforms which were very much comprehensive covering almost all aspects of economic life of the Indian Economy. It included strengthening of market forces, industrial and trade liberalization financial deregulations, privatization and foreign direct investment (FDI). The reforms had varying impact on different sectors, The education sector also came under its impact.

THE NIPFP, UNESCO, WORLD BANK AND XTH PLAN REPORTS ON H.E.

In 1997, the National Institute of Public Finance and Policy (NIPFP) prepared a paper on the provision of subsidies. This discussion paper classified secondary and higher education as a "non-merit good". Only elementary education was considered as a "merit good". Hence govt. as recommended should reduce subsidies on higher education. The approach paper towards HE came under severe attack from noted economists and educationists. Consequently the Ministry of Finance partly modified its earlier classification of goods. It put HE into a category called "Merit –2 goods" which need not be subsidized by the state at the same level as merit goods. The approach paper to the Xth Plan notes: " Since budget resources are limited and as such resources are available, need to be allocated to expand primary education. It is important to recognize that the universities must make greater effort to supplement resources from the Govt. University fees are unrealistically low and in many universities have not been raised it in decades. A substantial hike in universality fees is essential (Xth plan Approach Paper: 2001). A " Policy Framework for Reforms in Education" as a part of Prime Minister's Council on Trade and Industry of the then NDA Govt. was made. This report recommended that Govt.'s role should be 'maximum' in the sphere of primary education but 'minimum at the level of higher education. This report is popularly known as Ambani -Birla report. It is also recommended that all educational institutions in India -Schools, Colleges and Universities and other institutions of HE must be rated by independent agencies as is the case with financial sector. It is also strongly recommended that the funding should be linked to the rating earned by the educational institutions. The change in the govt. attitude could be attributed to the reports of UNESCO and the World Bank that social rates of return are found to be consistently higher than private rates of return to education. Hence it was recommended that public subsidies could be reduced and individual could be asked to pay for their education and private returns of HE are more than those of primary and secondary education (World Bank: 1994, 2000) It has been estimated that social return of primary education is 25 percent while HE is only one percent.

OBSERVATIONS AND FINDINGS

It is also argued that subsidization of HE would be regressive leading to income inequalities by transferring resources from poor to rich , as benefits of higher education accrue more to rich than to poor. Resource Chrunch is the fundamental problem at Govts. in developing countries. Education is the only sector where expenditure can be reduced to a certain extent in the context of resource chrunch.

Privatisation is the catchword at present in HE. It is not bad per se. However its application to education would be highly injurious and inequitous in Indian context. 'Pay as you consume' no doubt is the golden maxim if private sector is allowed to occupy more space in education. Equity and social justice demand that the beneficiary of primary and secondary education from deprived and weaker sections should have access to HE. Those who are able to pay must pay but what about the millions who are unable to pay? if market forces and principles are applied to the provision of education, then meritorious students from economically disadvantageous groups women and minorities may be compelled to pull themselves out. The western model in the area of education finances cannot be taken as an example for India.

THE URGENT NEEDS AND VALUABLE SUGGESTIONS

Following suggestions are vital, instrumental and ear marked as proper concomitant and commitment for the improvement of education in general and HE in particular. These are the urgent needs as detailed below:

- Quantitative expansion of mushrooming growth of HE institution should be checked and in its place maintaining of high quality is the need of the time,
- Restructuring, refining and modernizing the

existing system of education should be made to meet the new challenges and needs of the present time.

- Making higher education most cost effective, first the unit cost is to be accounted for,
- Meeting the challenges of HE in international considerations.
- Managing Colleges and Universities at a democratic level.
- Earmarking Budgetary provisions, its extension to 30 percent instead of 10 percent, differential fee structures should be made.
- Filling up the vacant posts with immediate effect.
- Higher secondary education's bifurcation from higher education.
- Induction of electronics media for Higher Education and Research Programmes and its induction be immediately made.
- Privatization of HE, greater investment of funds and introduction of self financing courses and use of computers are the immediate actions and tasks ahead for bringing structural reforms in the field of education.

CONCLUSION

To sum up steps should be taken to harmonize education as an easy access to the worthy and deserving scholars in our society who should take a vow to serve the mankind after being educated and also for the greater interest of the society and humanity at large. Pioneering efforts be made and developed to cater to the need of the nation in toto and to achieve many fold progress in all spheres HE. its development depends on the development of primary education. Its investment is made for investment in next generation. The state should bear the cost for it. He should not be at present a silver spoon feed meal rather it should be a sweet dream of masses.

REFERENCES

1. Ambani M. and K. Birla (2001): *Report on a Policy framework for Reforms in Education*, GOI, New Delhi.
2. Govt. of India (2001): *Approach paper to Xth Five Year Plan, 2002-2007.*Planning Commission, New Delhi.
3. Srivastava D.K. and Sen Tapas K. (1997*): Govt. subsidy in India*, NIPFP, New Delhi.
4. EPW (2004): *Public subsidies in Education in India,* No. 4; Jan 24.
5. Dougherty, K. (2004): *Financing HE in U.S. structure.*
6. WTO (1998) *Education services Its Background.*
7. World Bank (1994): *HE the Lessons of Experiences,* Washington. D.C.

4

Global Education and India

Sri Sidhartha Sankar Rath

Lecturer in History, U.N.S. Mahavidyalaya, Khairabad, Mugpal, Jajpur –755009, (Orissa)

Globalisation is the result of the Pursuit of economic opportunities of the scientific and technologically advanced nations especially the U.S.A. The concept or philosophy of globalisation sounds good. There is going to be larger integration of world economy. Money will flow from the rich countries to the undeveloped. Also there will be the free flow of ideas, technologies, goods and people. The world will be one village. Whatever may be its repercussions on the poor farmers or students or on the social institutions but in the broader sense our economy is rising, national foreign currency reserve is increasing, MNCs are opening their industrial set up here. Indian industrialists are increasingly getting space in world market. But this age is witnessing the revival of Indian spiritualism. The so called Yoga gurus, Ramdev, Ravi Sankar, Asharam bapu etc are carrying out an awakening movement and we are reaping the benefit in the IT and management sector where Indian students are doing well. Brain drain problem is over now and we are gradually establishing our own supremacy in the knowledge sector or in other words we can say knowledge economy is our asset or strength to get global recognition. To sum up Indian knowledge industry has tremendous potential to become a super power in technology, management, IT also in yoga and Ayurveda. Knowledge sector is the only one field where globalisation can be beneficial to world people.

Education is one of the Services covered under GATS as marketing. Education now-a-days is a more profitable proposition with very great potentials and possibilities. Free unfettered trade in education seems to be imminent. The educational system of all the countries of the world are to be opened up as per GATS mandate. Therefore education must possess in built quality and saleable skills while competing with other best trades of the world.

WTO classification list (w/120) divided educational services in five parts. Vig. (a) primary education services, (b) secondary services, (c) higher education services, (d) adult education (e) other educational services (professional, technical etc) India being one of the founding members of the WTO can not close its door to globalisation of education. Dr. V.B. Shastri in his paper "Challenges of Globalisation to education and quality Imperatives" visualised that international trade in education under the globalisation scenario is likely to take place through four modes.

1) International Distance Education mode
2) Institutional collaboration of two or more countries.
3) Institutional presence directly or through a system of franchise

4) Trans-National Mobility of students and intellectuals /teachers.

In a globally competitive world India will be a loser in the international trade market, if quality and relevance are not in built, empowerment and status of the teachers are not enhanced, suitable infrastructure is not available, obsolete curriculum and courses are not properly substituted and revamped, research specially mass action researches are not strengthened, evaluation and monitoring are not in built. Without a world education the out flow of students will comparatively become more than the inflow along with more brain drain to brain gain. Thus in a globally competitive world, it is quality of education that can sustain a nation. Quality will produce knowledge and in the modem world knowledge is power.

To make education qualitative productive and globally competitive, the following suggestions should be implemented starting from primary education.

1) Language – Native & Foreign
2) Study of Humanities and Culture
3) Spiritual Teaching like Yoga and Ayurveda
4) Scientific, Technical, Managerial and Vocational Education.

We are living in an age of endless conflicts, competitions and challenges. The education system demands a proper fusion of the above. While importance should be given for imparting the study of native language and culture along with English at the primary level at the same time there should be the introduction of yoga and computer education to prepare the little students mentally and morally to shoulder responsibility of the nation in the future. Universal basic education is an absolute priority with emphasis on universal access and enrollment, universal retention of children up to 14 years of age should be undertaken.

Globalisation in the coming years will bring unprecedented opportunities and crisis among the educated youth. It will bring hopes and despair, open possibilities and close doors to many. Because this is the age of experts. The world will be looking for trained persons in all basic fields and with ability to adopt to new demands. Thus in present century all the curricular subjects not only science and technology, commerce, humanities even languages, vocational and professional will be demanded in newer context of marketing, consumerism, human resources, modern knowledge economy for business and multicultural integration. Hence higher education in the coming decades will become universal but selective with emphasis on employment generating courses. There will be a corresponding decline in the study of humanities because man will act as machines and become self oriented. There will be the erosion of social values, fellow feelings, moral responsibilities and no respect for culture and tradition. Enrolment in humanities will decline as we are witnessing today. Competition will be stiff among students to get admission in technical institutes. After 20 years number of skilled persons will rise but place of employment will remain static with the introduction of computers and roberts to work in industrial sector. So the mad race of experts will make social scenario more confused.

No doubt privatization in higher education with social audit will expand. Besides, the popular demand will force the government to open qualitative institutions. Cost of education will increase. Only 30% of the Indian meritorious students can afford to read in these institutions. The students of the haves families will reap the benefit. Exploitation in the name of quality education will increase. The example is Vedanta group, which is going to establish a world class university in Orissa with Rs. 15000 crores investment without any little respect to Orissan student, culture and study.

To ensure quality every institution should have a road map of its own. It must have a brand name and culture of its own. This road map must contain mission and vision, quality and policy details and programme of action supported by constant monitoring and review. To ensure quality, every institution should have sufficient infrastructure, learning resources, academic environment, competent dedicated teaching faculties, need based curriculum, use of technology and an effective system of management. To make it productive education system should add entrepreneurship to the syllabus and prepare students right from school and college stages for setting up enterprises which will provide them with creativity, freedom and ability to generate wealth. Additionally the spirit that we can do should be inculcated in the youth.

To conclude in the age of globalisation urgent steps need to be taken to curb deculturisation, dehumanization and alienation. To bring equality in the society and to give justice to the poor students of the nation there must be reservation of seats in the technical institutes for the talented poor students.

However, education doesn't believe in sermons. It needs functional and structural changes. We cannot close our door to external changes; rather educational system should adjust to the demand of the time.

5

Globalisation and Education Need of Curriculum for Lifelong Learning Programmes

Sri Basanta Kumar Panda

Department of Commerce: U.N.S. Mahavidyalaya, Khairabad, Mugpal, Jajpur–755009, (Orissa)

Globalization is a 'qualitatively new phenomenon' of multi-dimensional nature posing a variety of 'complex trends' in the economic, social and cultural fabrics of all societies. The above phenomenon and trends stemming from it have placed formidable challenges and changing demands of lasting consequences everywhere. Humanity is at cross roads now; almost all people feel powerless to check the proliferating effects. There is a bewildering mixture of uncertainty, risk, insecurity, division and yet opportunity. Millions of people move across borders in search of a better life, or any life at all. Globalization impacts on all conceivable facets of life, including education, rapid developments in technology and communication are forcing changes within educational systems across the world as ideas, values and knowledge, vital to education, cross nation states and boundaries. There should be a new social universe (Phrase used by Postone, 1996) in the days to come.

The World Trade Organization's (WTO) 'education agenda' is in the nature of facilitating penetration of education services by corporate capital. The key WTO agreement for this purpose, the General Agreement on Trade in Services (GATS) incorporates the aim of 'unleashing progressive liberalization of Trade in services including public services like education'. No area of social life would be exempted from the imminent 'businessification' due to the vortex of corporate capital penetration; the 'value –form of labour' (phrases used by Gelenn, 2002) would certainly be different than now. In the changed context of GLP (Globalization, Liberalization and Privatization), 'human labour becomes a commodity like all other commodities and is exchanged for wages'. Consequently, education services would naturally be commercialized, privatized and capitalized (CPC); education would soon be wearing a new face –'modernized' for a 'knowledge economy' based on information technologies. Its values, preferences and tastes would certainly be different. 'Old traditional modes of working, professional values, notions of public service, putting community needs before the drive for profit' would become obsolete in the context of market, competition and profit making trends.

It is certain that the dawn of the new age in India and elsewhere' will be characterized by unimaginable advances in knowledge and synthesis of knowledge, triggering major changes in the objectives, contents, and methods of higher education. The future of countries would be largely determined by their abilities to compete in a global market where industrial based economies are given way to knowledge based industries. 'The educational need in the post- industrial society of the present' is preparation for and involvement in life, not mere graduation. The needed preparation can be achieved by enabling our learners to acquire appropriate 'knowledge, skills and the intellectual capacity to meet the challenges of accelerated change and uncertainty.' The demand of the emerging global society from the enterprise of education is quicker, cost –effective production of 'global citizens'- intelligent people with a broad range of skills and knowledge' excellently equipped for employment in a competitive information based techno-driven environment.

THE INDIAN SCENE

The National Policy on Education (NPE) 1986 lamented on the poor equipments of education in our country, lambasted the defect of the existing system and charged the system pointing out that little consideration was given to the employability of university graduates and or the absorptive capacity of the job market. 'The apex body in charge of higher education in India - the University Grants Commission (UGC) took note of emerging demands for ' a whole range of new skills.... from the graduates of humanities, social sciences, natural sciences and commerce, as well as from the various professional disciplines. 'At the whipping of the NPE and acting on the understanding of realities, the UGC established Curriculum Development Cells (CDC) for 27 subjects mandating them for 'modernizing the courses and restructuring them into unit courses and to develop alternate models with emphasis on learning.' The UGC has also identified 35 vocational subjects with an 'emphasis on providing knowledge and skills required for entry into gainful employment, particularly self employment'. These are not enough.

Educational institutions are still playing an ambivalent role in manpower production. They should understand that the organized sector has only limited absorptive capacity and hence the need to concentrate on diversification to a very great extent; development of capabilities for not only self employment but also for venturing into informal sectors, up gradation of productivity of household occupations. Ours is the age of a techno-scientific revolution, the pace of change taking place in the work place 'requires people to re-equip themselves, as new knowledge and new skills are needed ... to compete, survive and prosper'. The forecast for Futurists is that a life long career in one organization is soon bound to become rare. People will require new knowledge and skills to control and manage their own working lives. If the present traditional pattern of education is continued 'sooner or later... countries will have to contend with one of the most explosive problems of discontent and frustration... of graduate unemployment.'. The warning statement is: 'More of the same'- will not suffice as a strategy for meeting today's challenges.'

It is happy augury that the Govt. of India is aware of the emerging trends. The presentation of the Country Paper by Union Minister for Human Resource Development, at the UNESCO Conference (1998) evidences such awareness. The Minister has acknowledged India's recognition of the new global scenario posing unprecedented challenges on the higher education systems of nations. Indicating the major objective for future education in India, the minister has underscored the need for Lifelong Education (LLE) and has declared that 'great emphasis will fall upon life long education and the realization of a learning society' in the country. We learn that UNESCO is also greatly inspired by the paradigm of 'Life Long Education' (LLE), which holds "the key that allows us to cross the threshold of the Twenty-first Century".

LIFELONG EDUCATION: WHAT IT MEANS?

The very phrase 'Lifelong Education' (LLE) appears to be puzzling and sounds rather vague. It is true that the expression has not yet really fired the imagination of the people at large, especially those not engaged in learning beyond educational institutions – at work, in the community, in their homes and families and in their leisure and recreational lives. To some people, the notion of 'LLE' may even sound like a penal sentence or endurance test than an invitation to pleasure, achievement and progress.

LLE is a very vast field defying any precise definition. The essence of LLE could be inferred from its salient characteristics: LLE aims to (i) constitute a continuous process of forming whole human beings – their knowledge and aptitudes, as well as the critical faculty and ability to act, (ii) enable people to develop awareness of themselves and their environment and encourage them to play their social role at work and in the community.

LLE ranges from the most highly formal and structured educational activities to the most informal and tentative explorations of understanding; LLE encompasses many different levels, purposes, contents, outcomes and motives for learning: LLE anticipates a great variety of learning styles and approaches and it celebrates diversity. Due to these features, LLE may even appear to be 'so all inclusive' that it inhibits sharpness of focus and so strategies to promote LLE may become multi standard where in the development of a clear sense of priority may get prevented. Still, as UNESCO sees it 'LLE holds the key, as people's needs of life long learning are constantly expanding.

LLE can not be the one imposed by any agency; it should happen as part of a learning culture, depending and thriving on a great variety of initiatives taken by many actors in many different spheres. The Government's role shall be to monitor and steer developments and redistribute resources so that opportunities are equitable, systematic, flexible and efficient. The very diverse, pluralistic and lifetime duration of LLE requires co-ordination among many policy sectors, involving both macroeconomic and structural policies.

Countries need to develop a new learning culture, a culture of life long learning for all. The culture of LLE is essential to help the country and all the people meet the challenges they now face in the wake of GLP. We have noted that the challenges crop from many different spheres of life, the economy and labour market competition and so on. They are evident in the demand for new products and services and in the radical and far-reaching transformations in technology, information and communications now in train. There are also wide ranging changes to be addressed in families, communities, and relationships and in people's aspirations and very identities.

RECOMMENDATIONS FOR DESIGNING CURRICULA FOR LIFELONG EDUCATION

The output of the university education process, as of now at the first level, is a graduate with a degree qualification and certain abilities, which should qualify him or her for activities in the industry sector. It has been emphasized earlier that the level and skills profile should be relevant to the labour market requirements. Therefore **the learner/graduate qualification should be described as a set of abilities required to exercise the profession, rather than just listing the knowledge acquired in the education process**. To identify the set of abilities required for each programme and to define learner outcomes from the programmes, the main stakeholders here – the College/University professors, representatives from the profession (e.g. industry), industrial and professional associations, accreditation bodies, government, and also the students should have regular channels of communication. A valuable input for defining the outcomes of curricula would be the core Generic Skills Profiles (GSP), for each programme that have to be formulated and established by the stakeholders.

For designing useful curriculum and undertaking it as a continuous process, active Working Groups (WG) or Curriculum Development Cells (CDC) in each IHE should be constituted. The WG/CDC should aim at providing scope for vast flexibility, reflecting needs in curriculum for change, broad basing of skills, business knowledge, behavioural skills, more mobility etc. There should be a clear perception in the minds of curriculum makers of what competencies do learners need for successful performance in industry/user systems? (technical, professional and personal competencies) and what knowledge should be taught?

The planners should study existing curricula by involving user representatives (industry) to identify gaps (skill requirement) and formulate content outlines. It is a fact that there is no one single way to design the best curriculum. One can find one's own best solution; nevertheless, a framework based on experience and best practices can lead to a set of useful guidelines.

CLEARLY DEFINED CURRICULUM

The curriculum defines the Education Process (the sequence of adjusted lecturers and exercises which deliver knowledge), the Examination Process (which evaluates the students achievements), and the Training Process (which helps practice these skills and develop abilities). The college/university curriculum should aim to bridge the gap between the input and output requirements. An ideal curriculum is strictly focused on outcomes, lifting the students' qualification from entry to a clearly defined exit/output (graduate) level. The qualification process has to be defined with out any ambiguity.

KNOWLEDGE CYCLE IMPLICATIONS

The cycle of knowledge creation, distribution, learning and utilization is becoming shorter. This in turn leads to a need for continuous qualification of the workforce and an update of the learning content. As a result, new curricula reflecting novel content, learning objectives, teaching methodology, certification and relevant learning process need to be designed. These curricula should meet the needs of traditional full time learners as well as non traditional learners such as part timers and mature students. In order to meet all these requirements the new curricular need a highly flexible structure on a modular basis so that they can be easily adapted to different target groups, different skills profile needs and the rapid pace of change.

QUALITY CONTROL

IHES should set up a quality control process; the findings/ results shall be documented and the information gleaned should be applied to the further improvement of the programme. Such a process should take feedback from the student in terms of how well the course matched outcome objectives and whether the student felt he or she got the right knowledge and skills for the job from the course. The quality control process should also get feedback from industry in assessing the former students competencies in both technical and behavioural areas. This requires following of learners' recruitments in user-systems. (for graduate/undergo specific training and to their employer sometime between one and three years later.).

CO-ORDINATION

The quality of the educational process depends hugely on co-ordination between the sub-processes as well as between the protagonists (internal and external) involved and the feedback loops put in place at all levels. The internal protagonists in all these processes are students, professors and other academic and administrative staff. Externally, industry representatives are involved whenever students spend the placement period, work on these or work in industry during holiday periods. Co-ordination between all the players is to be ensured without any breakdown.

CURRICULUM STRUCTURE

In general, no curriculum can prepare students for activities at expert level in all skill profiles. However, every LLE curriculum should provide a common platform at basic level, enabling the learners to work in teams on common projects and to communicate in common LLE language even if they have specialized in different sectors.

The curriculum for LLE programmes shall consists of hierarchically organized modules: sets of core modules; sets of **area specific core modules; sets of optional (elective) modules.**

- **The core modules** represent the Scientific and Technology Base giving the fundamentals and basis for all LLE skills profiles. They represent also the slow changing knowledge. A selection from these modules is recommended to be scheduled during the first year/phase of study.
- **The area specific core modules** represent the technological base which are specific for the technological area of the group of core skill profiles targeted and they represent the faster changing knowledge. It is suggested that they be scheduled in the second or later years of study.
- **The elective modules** reflect the fastest changing knowledge with a period of ageing of this knowledge of 3-5 years. They reflect the novel technological and other specific knowledge. These modules are used to provide a specialized and in depth approach and to equalize the differences, thus giving a flexibility and possibility to specialize in certain areas.

Along with all the above listed skills, Personal and Business skills shall also be developed during the entire study, starting in the first semester. Primarily they should be integrated into the teaching of technical/applied subjects. Where additional modules are necessary, they should follow the same structure as the technical knowledge area. This structure can be applied for curricula leading to both first (UG) and second (PG) degree taking into account that all the modules in a second-degree programme should be designed at an advanced level.

DISTRIBUTION

A basic knowledge of chosen subject is essential for a broad understanding of further processes and their utilization in technical applications; however it also serves as a foundation for attaining a breadth and depth of knowledge in a specialist field of application. A broad foundation is also an important prerequisite to enable graduates to communicate effectively with colleagues from other areas using a common 'technical language. ' So, the core of qualifications to be attained during education should comprise a **scientific base and a technology base** i.e. a broad spectrum of mathematical, scientific and technical knowledge; **application base/systems thinking and personal and business skills.**

This core should extend to all subjects under consideration, thus laying the foundation for subsequent professional mobility. The teaching of this core need not be at a deeper level but should give students a balanced overview. The following distribution between **STAP** (**Scientific, Technological bases and Application and Personal business skills**) has been suggested.

The Scientific base: This aims to cover the fundamental principles relevant to the concepts used in the industry/establishment. In addition to a foundation in science and mathematics, the scientific base should foster an understanding of scientific methods for analysis and design. The percentage suggested for this segment is 30%.

The Technology base: This is more concern with giving a broad overview of the various technologies available, the functions they can perform and their advantages and constraints. In addition to studying the current capability of a technology, students should be given some insight into how that technology might develop in the future. For this segment also a 30% distribution is suggested.

Application Skills: A command of the basics is not in itself sufficient for assuring professional competence in industry. In order to meet the demands of the job, graduates also need an in-depth fundamental knowledge of their specialized fields, general knowledge of problem solving methods, and finally particular application knowledge in accordance with workplace demands for the particular job profile. The key requirements here are knowledge of system functions in the field in question, and understanding of the technological possibilities ('hardware and software') to realize or implement those functions with the help of procedural methods. Given the growing complexity of modern devices, equipment and systems, the ability to see things as a whole, to think in terms of systems and to communicate a systems level with all those working on the project and with the customers is increasingly important. It is suggested that this segment can have a distribution at 25%.

Personal and Business Skills: These skills have to be developed through team projects, commercial simulations, negotiation, presentations etc. throughout the course. Coupling this implicit learning with feedback and coaching from lecturers not only on the academic aspects, but on how well these skills are acquired and deployed should provide the on going learning stimulus needed to develop these skills which are vital for a career. Particular attention should also be paid to embedding the teaching of these essential personal and business skills, into the more technical subjects area. The suggested percentage for this segment is 15% Apart from the above, the curriculum should have provision for **Practical/Work experience and Project Work.**

PRACTICAL/WORK EXPERIENCE IN LLE PROGRAMMES

A minimum of three months (or longer, for longer programmes) is necessary to emphasize the connections between different aspects, to encourage a broad systems view and to illustrate the practical, technological and human constraints of solving real world problems.

PROJECT WORK

Project work is vital to develop the skills listed above and it is recommended that at least three months be allocated for the project and the dissertation. It is recognized that there are difficulties in assessing the performance of individual students when team projects are being undertaken. Nevertheless, some experience of team working on a significant real project is an essential element of a good education. The challenge of assessing and crediting teamwork by students needs to be addressed by academia. The industry has developed means of assessing and improving group works of its workforce. Academia might benefit from this industry experience of assessment of these skills.

RECOMMENDATIONS FOR IMPLEMENTING LLE

No country like India could afford to continue the model of general education as it has been persisting in for the large bulk of the student population. A major change and investment is required to make human resource productive by coupling the older general disciplines of humanities, social sciences, natural sciences and commerce to their applications in the new economy. Out efforts shall be directed to provide for adequate field based experience to enhance knowledge with skills and develop appropriate attitudes. While preparing for this tremendous task, it may be helpful to take guidance from Aurobindo: **The past is our foundation, the present our material, the future our aim and summit. Each must have its due and natural place in a national system of education".**

- Higher education itself is a complex process. The challenges posed by the present time are bound to increase the complexity of the system that performs the sacred function of preparing the next generation. The system has to reconcile with the new awakening that all knowledge is interdisciplinary and no more compartmentalized, department/teacher centerd, fossil courses could be justified and sustained. Multi/ Cross disciplinary programmes in frontier developments in subjects and work areas with constantly renewed, updated curriculum have to be planned and implemented.
- It would not be enough if the Institutions of Higher Education (IHE) – colleges and Universities – continue the age –old long term (2 yrs/3yrs) degree programmes and attempt tinkering with them by introducing some vocational components here and there at the first degree level or elsewhere. Even after leaving the college, the learner could be proved with opportunities to come back for renewal and updating of knowledge

and sharpen his skills for new work situations. IHEs should turn to become vibrant centres to provide opportunities for their alumni and other members of the society unending opportunities 'to renew, update and widen their knowledge and skills throughout life'. Suitable curriculum for such further educational opportunities needs to be evolved in close collaboration with user systems.

- In the new situation of GLP and CPC environment, the conventional modes of delivery may not be of much use; there should be more of evening, part-time, flexi-time programmes (including week end/holiday courses) for a vast array of varying requirements of different segments of the society, for people who wish to learn new job skills; for people seeking advanced knowledge/skills / degrees in their own specialities; for people simply wanting to improve their minds/ developing new interests or just to know more; for people in transition/ migration from jobs; for people rendered jobless due to technological changes from obsolete jobs and skills and so on. It would even be worthwhile to think of certain programmes under a combination of distance and direct modes of delivery providing more flexibility for the learners.
- Ready access and flexibility shall be the hallmarks of LLE initiatives. At the same time, flexibility shall never be at the cost of quality. All short duration; flexi time programmes would be designed to ensure highest quality and relevance for specific, current and projected needs of user systems.
- The programmes shall be designed under interactive modular patterns/framing. The learner

should be free to choose any module and get appropriate training therein and earn due credits for each module he /she completes. She/he should also have the freedom to complete requirements for any degree/ diploma etc suiting his/her own pace of study and or convenience. Accumulation of earned credits from different modules of learners' choice and transfer of credits to fulfill degree/diploma requirements should be permitted. It would not be out of place to think of allowing credit transfer from other institutions, universities and also from distance education modes. The cafeteria approach that permits such flexible credit transfers shall be implemented in our IHES.

- The quality of the outcome of higher education is generally measured based on the learners' success in profession / life situations. The success of the learners depends on different stakeholders inside and outside the IHES. In order to become successful, IHEs have to necessarily involve all the key players from the beginning in the design, control and operation of this process. Such a need has been stated earlier and repeated here to point out the imperative that educational institutions should forge excellent linkages with industries and major user -- organisations and embark upon joint efforts in curriculum planning, providing hands on shop floor experience, testing of laboratory findings/ products, funding chairs, projects, research, infrastructure etc.
- Generally entrants to the higher education (i.e. at the UG level) have qualification profile and level acquired though the higher secondary education up to the age of 17-18 years. Second level (PG) courses will normally build on a first level degree.

The key players in the scene College/University professors, high and higher secondary school teachers, and departments for education, learners and their parents should organize permanent functioning communication links amongst them for improving performance of the higher secondary education process (that precedes the university education process) and increasing the ability of first year students to respond well to the objectives of the curriculum of the College/University/LLE.

- The days of Open University System – allowing persons to sit for university degree examinations without insisting upon earlier qualifications except age requirements- have come to stay in our educational framework. The Open system should be extended further to cover all courses/ degrees/ programmes insisting only on specific knowledge, skills and abilities, instead of any formal earlier qualification. The required knowledge/skill level should be specified and should be such that could be tested easily at the entry level. The entry requirements of expectations should reflect the institutional policy and the goals of the programme.

To make any programme a success, there should be, amongst other things like resources, infrastructure, adequate planning, necessary preparedness and commitment on the part of institutions and key players, a conducive environment for innovation and experiment and above all a determination to go ahead and reach goals for common good. The stakes are high in Education in the new situation (GLP) and climate (CPC). Hope now lies with education, the chief enterprise through which we can prepare the present for the future. Awake, Arise and Act.

Globalisation : The Emerging Trends in Higher Education

Sri Artta Bandhu Jena

Lecturer , P.G. Department of Business Management,
F.M. University, Balaosre.

"Gradually the diffusion of intelligence caused learning and talent to become a means of government, mental ability led to social power and the men of letters took a part in the affairs of the state."

TOCQUEVILLE

Democracy in America

INTRODUCTION

Noble Laureate Joseph Stiglitz defines globalisation as "removal of barriers to free trade and the closer integration of national economies (stiglitz, 2002. p.ix.). In other words, economic globalisation refers to the integration of different economies of the world through trade, investments and migration of people. The revolution in information technology and communication has rendered education portable, flexible, non-linear and student-centric. Globalisation in education refers to integrating an international dimension into teaching, learning and service functions of the institution. The concept of "quality assurance" is based on the western parameters or formulations. The management view of quality implies the quality of features and characteristics of product or service that bears on its ability to satisfy stated or implied needs. (Mohanty and lakhe, 2000. p.2). In Indian tradition, quality in education encompasses not only a product and a process, but thought as well. Quality education means the transformation of individual and society to higher physical, intellectual, aesthetic, moral and spiritual attainment.

ELITE BIAS IN HIGHER EDUCATION

The term higher education in India refers to post-secondary (Post –plus two) or tertiary level education. All institutions imparting instruction leading to a University degree or an equivalent may be termed as institutions of higher education. Higher education in India has expanded tremendously during the post independence period. At present, higher education in India is a gigantic sector, employing a large number of personnel, incurring an annual expenditure of millions rupees and teaching a large body of students. Education has played an important role in preparing men for life in society and moulding them accordingly whether directly or indirectly, overtly or covertly. No socio-political system can forgo securing its foundations by manning over minds and hearts to the principles, ideas, and common references and beyond these, the myths that bind a nation together.

Although India has had a long tradition of institutions of higher learning, exemplified amongst others, by the universities of Nalanda and Taxila, the system of higher education is vogue to-day, essentially dates back to the middle of the last century. In a way the establishment of the 3 universities in the 3 residency towns of Bombay, Calcutta and Madras, following the wood's dispatch of 1854, laid the foundation of the present day university education in India. The period of decolonisation in Asia, Africa and Latin America also considered with period of high optimism about the role of education in the socio economic transformation of economics. It was in this context that reforms in education were accorded a very high priority in independent India. Realizing the crucial role of human resources in development processes and their interface with education, a number of specific provisions and directives relating to the formation of human capital have been included in the constitution of India.

HIGHER EDUCATION IN INDIA

At present there are around 247 universities and 98 Deemed to be universities, more than 16 thousand colleges, 97 lakh students and 4.5 lakh teachers in India. When India becomes independent, there were just 18 universities, 500 colleges, 2,28 lakh students and about 25 thousand teachers. These figures shown in Table I gives impression that massive expansion of higher education has taken place after 1947. However, it is not completely true.

Table 2 shows the number of universities in some of the leading countries along with their population. Japan for its 12.7 crore people has 684 universities. USA with 27.6 crore population has 2364 universities. In UK and Germany there are 104 universities (in addition to 231 autonomous institutes) and 330

Table 1. Some basic Information on Higher Education in India

Sl.No.		1947	2003-04
1.	Universities	18	345
2.	Colleges	500	16000
3.	Students	228804	9463821
4.	Teachers	<0.24 lakh	4.36 lakh
5.	Budget	55 crores	>78000 crores

universities whose populations are 5.58 and 8.2 crores respectively. However, as mentioned above, for 100 crore Indians, we have only 345 universities. These facts are indicative of the acute shortage of universities in India and need to establish more to provide access to higher education particularly to people from rural areas. To come close to Japan and USA roughly we need 6000 to 9000 universities in India.

Table 2. Number of Universities in Some Leading Countries

Sl. No.	Country	Population (crore)	Universities
1.	Japan	12.7	684
2.	USA	27.6	2364
3.	UK	5.98	104 (231 Autonomous Institutes)
4.	Germany	8.2	330
5.	India	100	247+98 deemed to be universities

Table 3 shows the students enrollment in higher education in India with some selected leading countries. India is far behind with other countries. In India, it is a matter of great concern that most of them (approximately 94%) have no access to higher education and they are out of higher education. The main objective of UGC during tenth plan is to raise enrollment in higher education from present 6% to 10% by the end of the plan period. It would be great achievement, if we succeed in enhancing the enrollment by 3 to 4% by the year 2008.

Table 3. Students Enrollment in Higher Education in Some Selected Countries

Sl.No.	*Country*	*Percentage of Enrollment*
1	Canada	88
2	Australia	79.8
3	USA	80.9
4	UK	52
5	Thailand	19
6	Brazil	12
7	Indonesia	11
8	India	6

HIGHER EDUCATION AND ECONOMIC GROWTH

There is a close relationship between education and economy in all historical periods. We had to fight to procure just enough food for our consumption, education consisting of traditional knowledge and skills was passed on from generation to generation in non systematic manner. When increased production lead to the availability of leisure for at least some people, more formal schooling came into existence. Already education had become a means of maintaining the existing structure and cultural pattern of society. Economic growth, however, is not just increased production alone. Economic growth means more employment opportunities, increased productivity and social welfare; reduction of poverty and increase in standard of living. It has become a major goal of all developing countries to-day. They need especially of higher education to achieve above economic growth objectives. Higher education contributes many things for development from different angles i.e. agricultural, polity, science, and technology business etc. Thus, economic studies are available to show that in the long run, every rupee spent on education brings greater returns than a rupee invested elsewhere. In this context of Indian education, a clear policy statement in the National Policy on Education says that the education is an investment in the future of the nation.

PRIVATE PARTICIPATION IN HIGHER EDUCATION

Private institutions increased dramatically in many Asian and African countries from 1980s. Private institutions have become an integral part of higher education. Private participation started much earlier in Latin American countries. China reported to have more than 800 private higher education institutions. It has now a record of nearly a quarter century. At present the government and government aided colleges and University departments also run in self-financing programmes. Developing and developed countries are much favourable towards mass higher education. These countries aim at a substantial increase in the age group entering higher education.

The government drafted a Private Universities (Establishment and Regulation) Bill in 1995. This Bill was drafted for anticipating rightly, a significant role for private initiative in higher education. The Bill was introduced in both house of parliament, but there were reservations among members of the Loka Sabha. It is unfortunate that a good beginning made was not carried to its fruition. Again in 1999 the Ministry of Human Resource Development (HRD) set up a 6 members committee. This committee made a number of useful suggestions for reforming the higher education system and encouraging in a meaningful way the private domain of higher education. It was also suggested the enactments of the Private Universities Bill and amendments to the UGC Act. These recommendations have not been acted upon and the status quo-continues. In general, it may be stated that government need the complement of private institutions and the concept of parents paying for the education of their wards in full or in part has come to be accepted.

GLOBALISATION AND ITS IMPACT ON HIGHER EDUCATION

After independence there has been an improvement in the economic development of the country, there has been steady development in the international business atmosphere. Globalisation also has had an appreciative effect on the Indian business and as such, in order to keep pace with the fiercely competitive atmosphere, it is essential to adopt changes, which in turn requires suitable adjustments/ changes in higher education. The demand of education on the basic subjects has almost reached the saturation point and there is steady decline in demand for the existing higher education of the 21st century. Due to the changing times and the cut throat competition, the importance of the present trend of higher education has depleted. As such also, it is all the more necessary that changes are introduced in the higher education system and adopting ourselves to the changing scenario, in consonance with local needs in the 21st century.

To-day India has second largest education system in the world after the United States. The year 1991 is considered to be the major turning point for higher education sector in India. The World Bank in its document titled "Higher Education: **The Lessons of Experience** in 1994 states that higher education is of paramount importance for economic and social development. Institutions of higher education have prime responsibility for equipping individuals with advanced knowledge and skills required for positions of responsibility in government, business and professions. It considers the involvement of private sector in higher education in order to achieve the objectives of quality and access in the long run. India being a member of WTO, is supposed to open up its higher education sector to international competition in the present era of privatization, liberalization and globalization. The debate is towards the privatization of higher education due to various reasons taking into its benefits and shortcomings in education sector.

Globalization no doubt, promises dramatic and rewarding change to higher education systems of the developed countries. The present era may be called an academic globalization as the number of students aspiring and seeking foreign education is increasing. With the increasing globalization of economies, the globalization of higher education is inevitable. The debate at present is what is or should be the extent of globalization and not whether or not there should be globalization. The Debate is on privatision or globalization is mainly revolving around two main issues, Viz., **"Trading of Education"** and **"Role of Education".** The protagonists of both the schools of thought have strong arguments. Without having the clear understanding of both the perspectives, it is not possible to develop any rational policy framework. Above all, the privatization or globalization of higher education should be affordable to the all sides as a whole and to the individual, market and local needs of the developing country like India. Arthur Levine has identified 6 forces as mainly responsible for the worldwide spread of privatization in higher education. These are:

i. The rise of an information based economy.

ii. An increase in public scrutiny

iii. A decline in public trust in the government.

iv. The advent of new technologies

v. The convergence of knowledge based organizations and

vi. Demographic changes.

The first four of these are applicable. But the dynamics of globalization or privatization in higher education is no doubt a challenge as well as an opportunity, Yet, the matter of the fact is, this access remains only as availability. Who can reach to it and how? What alternative provisions are made for those who cannot afford to reach is the crux of the matter.

TENTH FIVE YEAR PLAN (2002-07)

The Tenth Five Year Plan sets objectives to increase student enrollment of the Indian population in the age group (18-23) in the higher education from the existing 6% to 10% by the end of the plan that is 2007. Table 3 shows the student enrollment in higher education in some selected countries. Student enrollment in higher education in India is far below as compared to western countries. The government are to take more strategies to bridge the gap with western countries to increase the student enrollment in higher education in India. Some strategies are made for better student enrollment in higher education under the existing 10th plan. These strategies are as follows:

I. Increasing access
II. Quality of education
III. Adoption of the state specific strategies.
IV. Globalization and liberalization of higher education system.
V. Relevance including course curriculum
VI. Vocational and distance Education
VII. Convergence of formal and Non-forma education
VIII. IT Education Institutions etc.

The existing plan also entails increased private participation in higher education and meeting the challenges in the area of internalization of Indian higher education.

CONCLUDING REMARKS

Here, some concluding remarks from the above discussions are as follows:

I. Higher education should include both, personality development and job training.
II. In the present era of globalization, liberalization and privatization there is a need for devoting deep thought to higher education. Higher education shall be relevant in the 21st century.
III. Higher education should be need based so that the student can be given the proper direction in life.
IV. As products of the higher education or ITR institution have to face the future challenges, there is an urgent need for frequent revision of course curriculum in consultation with the industry.
V. Creating a proper and purposeful interaction between university, government, industry and

society.

VI. India has to learn from itself and search a way out from within to truly integrate educational aspects with the global society.

VII. In the era of globalization, only upper section (rich) of society are enjoying the fruits of higher education. further, governmental plans, policies and its implementation toward globazlization or privatization should be in such way that dominant minorities viz. STs, SCs, OBCs, Muslims etc., those who are poor they shall not be affected.

VIII. As compared to other leading countries population, there should be more universities in India to meet the present as well as future challenges.

IX. The budget allocation should be more in every financial year to increase the student enrollment in higher education in India.

X. The more and more trained teacher should be appointed in higher education. Proper infrastructure should be provided.

XI. Change in any sphere is nothing new. Private sector (both Indian and foreign) investments in higher education should be encouraged. But the objectives of higher education in India shall not be affected.

REFERENCES

1. *Higher Education: Retrospectives and Prospects* – Indira Gandhi National Open University.
2. *Planning and Management of Higher Education: A Macro – Perspective.* Indira Gandhi National Open University.
3. *Strategy.* The Journal of Management Development, Dec. 2006, Berhampur University, Orissa.
4. **Survey of Indian Industry** – The Hindu –2006.

5. - The Indian Journal of Commerce, April - September 2003.
6. - University News 44 (33) August 14-20, 2006.
7. - University news 39 (35) August 27 –September 2, 2001
8. - University News 44 (19) May 8-14, 2006.

7

Emerging Trends in Education in the Age of Globalisation

Dr Sudhansu Sekhar Mishra
Reader in Commerce,
U.N.S. Mahavidyalaya, Khairabad,
Mugpal, Jajpur, 755009 (Orissa)

Anita Kumari
Research Scholar, Deptt. of Commerce,
BHU, Varanasi ,UP.

Education is the key to the development of any society. It provides many opportunities to develop skills in addition to the knowledge it creates. In developing countries the primary objective of education was to increase the percentage of literates. Therefore, every country has developed its own system of education to promote its socio-cultural identity. However, as the countries progressed the aims of education shifted from literacy to quality and applicability of education in society and its contribution towards the development of the country increased. In the present scenario quality has become the touchstone in all walks of life and so in the education sector the focus has been shifted from quantity to quality. Our country has reached a stage in its economical and technical development when major emphasis must be made on issues from which maximum benefit can be derived. This benefit must be derived from assets which have been already created. Education has a major role to play in doing so. However, the system of education in our country needs to undergo a major upheaval so as to meet the challenges of changing times.

Globalisation is the emerging reality of the twenty-first century. There exists today a global arena because of rapid advances made in Science and Technology in which the destiny of every individual is to some extent played out. We have become a worldwide community living in global village. The economic, scientific, cultural, political and knowledge interdependence dictated by opening up under the pressure of free trade theories of World Trade Organization (WTO) and General Agreement on Trade in Services (GATS)

The General Agreement on Trade in Services (GATS) is an agreement between countries who are signatories to the World Trade Organisation (WTO). Education is one of the services covered under GATS as marketing of education" is now a-days a more profitable proposition with very great potentials and possibilities. It is included under 12 classified sectors covering 161 services. The education system of all the countries of the world is to be opened up as per GATS mandate. Therefore, education must possess inbuilt quality and saleable skills while competing with other best trade of the world.

As far as the education system in India is concerned, it is globally competitive. India will be a loser in the international educational trade market if quality and relevance are not built, empowerment and status of the teachers are not enhanced, suitable infrastructure is not available, obsolete curriculum and courses are not properly substituted and revamped, research are not strengthened and evaluation and monitoring are not in built. Without a world-class education, the outflow of students will comparatively become more than the inflow along with more brain drain. Thus in a globalisation era, the quality of education that can sustain a nation will produce knowledge persons. So it is said that "Knowledge is power".

In order to fulfill the educational and informational functions successfully, universities need to respond effectively to the chainging education and training pattern. Institutions are transforming themselves to respond for evolving educational needs, particularly in the context of globalisation and a borderless market. New firms of competition and changing information and communication technologies emerge as part of this. In response to this need, the universities need to change some of the following aspects.

- Restructuring of general education courses
- Flexibility and course duration
- Changing Technology
- Industrial linkages.
- Transparency in Evaluation.
- Value –based Education
- Research perspective in Higher Education.

RESTRUCTURING OF GENERAL EDUCATION COURSES

The restructuring of courses should be focused on (i) social value formation through courses on science and society, contemporary problems of Indian development, national integration, social problems causes and remedies (ii) developing required knowledge through different course combinations like Physics, Mathematics, Computer Science, Economics, Insurance etc. (iii) developing abilities to apply knowledge through applied courses under different disciplines. Attempt is being made to develop skills through job-oriented courses which are likely to be demanded in job situations.

It is also important that universities not only restructure the courses but build more flexible core curriculum and should offer different ways in which students can earn a degree. There should be a public debate about the kinds of knowledge, skills, and value needed to prepare today's students, from school through college for an era of greater expectations in every sphere of life.

FLEXIBILITY AND COURSE DURATION

In most of the colleges affiliated to the universities, there is absolutely no flexibility in the choice of subject combinations. Students are often forced to study the subjects which are not of their choice. Also every course is time bound, any delay in completing a Semester or academic year marks the students as a dropout. All students are compelled to complete a course and obtain a degree in the minimum time with no consideration for higher thinking and true learning.

CHANGING TECHNOLOGY

In the globalisation era of high technology a new revolution is taking place in the way of human access, learning and interaction. Therefore it is needless to say that in a consultation on Higher education, a peep into the myriad ways in which technology can enrich higher education is essential. Such technology includes different combinations like audio, video, computers, telecommunications which integrates music, text images, live action video, spoken voices and animations. However, there is a myth among teachers that modern technology would remove the teacher from the classroom. But as it appears teachers will be cast in new roles as learning coaches and motivators. Research indicates that it is more productive for students to work with technology in pairs or in groups rather than alone. They become active participants in the learning process, exercising many kind of intelligence in dynamic ways, spending more "Mind on task" and developing effective interpretation skills.

INDUSTRIAL LINKAGE

Higher education institutions should enter into partnership with local industrial communities for learning process, by offering courses of interest to the local industries. A part of the learning process of the students will then be in these places. Students will gain authentic learning experience from such partnership and the institution will strengthen localities also. Revenue will increase without increasing the infrastructure.

TRANSPARENCY IN EDUCATION

In the presently system, the method of evaluating students at the end of the year through a single examination needs a lot of introspection. This system leads to mugging notes and reproducing them at the time of examination, which proves to be memory test instead of ability. This system has encouraged many mal-practices like copying, leakage of papers, dishonest corrections and fake mark sheets. The teachers alone by continual observation of a spectrum of abilities of their students can evaluate their performance. Checks of various kinds are necessary and perfectly feasible in such a system, and if necessary the outsiders can be associated either directly with some seminars, tutorials or projects or indirectly, by reviewing the evaluation process.

VALUE BASED EDUCATION

The maxim " Character is destiny" held a singular attraction for Dr. S. Radhakrishnan , the great educationist, philosopher, statesman and a symbol of ideal teacher. Indian's destiny as a nation depended on the value system that the youth imbibed. He had said that we cannot build rightly with the wrong materials. It is imperative that the young men and women should be trained in the right ideals and values. The words "value" may mean the value of a thing in terms of utility and cost. It may refer to the quality of life based on accepted virtues of a civilized society. Both senses of the word must get incorporated as the basic spirit of higher education in India. Therefore, job-oriented and industrially useful courses must be value based, in both the senses of the word. What value is added on material plane must be based on the plane of actual life. Courses have to be designed and redesigned according to the expectations of the society and industries.

RESEARCH PERSPECTIVES IN HIGHER EDUCATION

Research generates a body of knowledge for designing functionally effective programmes of action in searching for solutions for professional problems encountered in implementing the designed programmme or activities. Research findings provide lessons and guidelines for programmes to learn from.

They enable the person to identify the strengths, weaknesses, gaps and useful lessons to improve upon. Conducting researches are important but equally important is an adequate utilization of research results.

CONCLUSION

The better quality in higher education lies on the shoulders of the teaching fraternity. A negative approach to education has become common. Dissatisfaction is expressed in every aspect, in terms of structure of education, with the functioning of educational institutions, behaviour and attitude of the students as well as teachers, which can be attributed to the slow and sluggish pace of reforms. However, a realistic view with healthy criticism and vigorous effort may set the arena for future actions. The positive contribution of education can not be denied. Thousands of doctors, engineers, scientists and other personnel having the highest competence are available. The products have proved their mettle not only in India but also in the world. Educational progress which is the foundation for capabilities of the youth are a result of development of courses and syllabi. Therefore an upgrading of syllabi, educational, materials and equipments are to be done. The possibilities are greater if only the problem is minutely examined and the actions are far sighted. Education in future days will be based on eight major dimensions i.e. Soul, Soil, Society, Skill, Science, Solidarity, Service and Survivals. The ultimate objectives will be to achieve Life Enrichment Education, Life Skill Education and Life Value Education.

REFERENCES

1. Renu, N. (2003); *Radhakrishna's reflections on Education,* University News. 41 (19)

2. Yadav, S.K (2003); *Research Perspective in Teacher's Education,* University News. 41(22) pp 3-6.

3. M. Lakshmi Narasaiah - *Promotion of Research in Higher Education,* University News, 44 (49) pp 1 –3.

4. Mohapatra P.C. – *Opportunities and Challenges to Higher Education,* University News, 45 (01) pp 1-4.

5. D' Souza Anjali – *Emerging Needs and Challenges of Higher Education.* 45 (03) , pp 13-17.

8

Quality Imperatives of Education in the Era of Globalisation

Dr. Jyotsna Sahoo
Sr. Lecturer in Education,
Radhanath I.A.S.E., Cuttack.

It has been well recognized that economic development depends largely on the level of education and training of the workforce. In the 21st century, which increased global migration and global trading, there education must be globalised to facilitate optimum communication and contribution of people to the global economy. In the coming decades, there will be a shift from teaching society to knowledge society advancing towards a learning society and ultimately to society of wisdom. Education will be one of the principal means available to foster a deeper and harmonious form of human development and thereby to reduce poverty, exclusion, ignorance, oppression and the war. The major focus will be a transition "from learning to be" to learning to become". We have already crossed the three waves — Agrarian, Industrial and Information. (Alvin Toffler) Coming Millennium will be marked by a generation of fourth wave (Maynard & Mehrtens) having profiles like respiritualisation and a responsive society (global Stewartship) with increasing aspects of globalization, accountability, information technology and assimilation of power of knowledge (GAIA) Education of the future will be based on four pillars "Learning to know/learn, Learning to do, learning to live together and learning to be."

Quality education is a package which means;

a) Conforming to comparable standards with innovative approach.

b) Fulfilling the academic intellectual requirements for the age, stage or phase of education with optimal degree of excellence.

c) Adequate capability to consistently cope with the demands of the world of work and scope for employability.

d) Development of innate qualities to optimum level.

e) Satisfying the stakeholders as per social expectation and requirement, to ensure quality.

The coming century dominated by globalizations will gear towards world-class education based on values. Steps will be taken to curb deculturisation, delimitisation and alienation. Knowledge gaps will be bridged through net working of institutions, growth of educational complexes and wider access to e -learning and continuing education.

- Great emphasis on academic freedom, curbing ivory tower mentality and remodeling and enriching the institutions (both content and pedagogy) to meet the learning needs of a constantly growing student population.
- Sharing of knowledge, intertwining of research

institutions to build up research capacity and fresh impetus to partnership to solve problems and generations of new knowledge will be geared up.

- Exchange of students and teachers, assistance in the communication system particularly on line system, pooling of research findings of the Universities and establishment of regional centers of excellence at the national and international level may be accelerated.
- Majority of the institutions will become autonomous and will prepare its own road map backed by social audit, public accountability and continuous assessment of teachers by outside agencies and stakeholders.
- To ensure quality, every institution should have a road map of its own. It must have a brand name and a culture of its own, sufficient infrastructure, learning resources, academic environment, empowered, competent dedicated teaching faculties with due status, need based curriculum design, etc.
- To face the effect of globalisation in the employment and labour market, machines replace human beings and expansion of supervision, managerial and organizational tasks, the need of skilled personnel and increased abilities in employees will be in demand.

Therefore the universities and Higher education institutions must continue to be in a position to meet the demands and thus must constantly adopt specialized courses of study to the need of the society.

A shift will be marked from national policy on education to international policy with flexibility.

National Frame Work of Curriculum to Global structure, National standard parameters to International standard parameters, National accreditation and assessment to international accreditation and assessment, National testing service to international testing service, National Minimum levels of learning to International standard, Traditional way of teaching to technotronic process, networking and growth of mobile teachers of eminence, National core curriculum to international core, and inter national goals of education for world peace will also evolve.

Internationalization of education involves, true exchange of personnel and technologies among countries. This exchange allows first hand experience and deeper understanding of other cultures, their values and approaches, which promote more tolerance, respect and appreciation of cultural differences. To prepare individuals and societies for the global economy of the twenty first century, education must erase the barriers preventing true – exchange of experience / information. To achieve this purpose education should;

- Increase the level of literacy of the world population so that all people can read, understand and use their own language.
- Expose students to other cultures, values to promote cross cultural understanding and tolerance of cultural differences.
- Foster the formation of international guidelines/ standards for various occupations and educational milestones to facilitate recognition of educational qualifications and knowledge experiences of people who have moved from their place of origin to contribute to other countries.

- Foster research linkage and collaboration among inter disciplinary teams of various regions of the world.
- Emphasize life long, continuing learning to knowledge and technologies.
- Promote critical thinking and adaptability to facilitate adaptation to a quick changing society.
- Formulate an international language for technologies.

Education in the coming century will be based on eight major dimensions – soul, soil, society, skills, science and technology, solidarity, service and survivals. The ultimate objectives will be to achieve Life Enrichment Education (LEE), Life Skills Education (SSE) and Life Value Education (LVE). Globalisation of education is a necessity to prepare individuals and societies for the next century when global enterprises, true partnerships and global migration will be prominent features.

REFERENCES

1. Raya, R. Prabhakar, (2001), *TQM for Higher Education,* Journal for All India Association for Educational Research (Vol-13 , 2nd March)
2. *Institutional Accreditation Manual for self appraisal of Teacher Education* (2005), NAAC.
3. Sen, S. *Towards Global Culture in Higher Education Institutions in India,* NAAC News, July 2005.
4. = Darial, John Sri. (2006). *Higher Education, Teacher Education, Distance Education, What is Quality and who says so* ? NAAC, News April 2006.
5. - *Programme of Action 1992 Ministry of Human Resource Development* Department, Govt. of India.
6. - *International Commission for Twenty First Century.*

9
Primary Education in the Era of Globalisation

Sri Premananda Pradhan
Lecturer in Economics, Science College,
Konkorada, Ganjam, Orissa 761144.

Education has been accepted as an important element of human resource development. It expands the mental horizon of the people. The physical, intellectual, emotional and ethical integration of the individual is not possible without it. It enriches the moral power of the civilized man. It provides the basic inputs to the modern men to be optimised. The constitution of India makes obligation for the state to provide free and compulsory education upto the age of fourteen. The recent 73rd constitutional amendment for universalisation of Elementary Education is a major step in this direction.

Success of a nation is determined by the quality of its citizens. Nation is not built by bricks and mortars but by the quality of men. It does not require any evidence to say that society and its development are positively co-related to the development of education.

The progress of Education in Orissa has been simultaneous with the movement for a separate state of Orissa in 1936. The centres of educational activity were the coastal districts of Cuttack, Puri and Balasore. Education in these districts received a boost because of missionary activities. Unfortunately, illiteracy was not only a big problem in post independent Orissa, poverty and natural calamities like floods, droughts and cyclones have been a constant concern of the Govt. of Orissa.

The growth scenario of primary education in Orissa is not satisfactory. The reason is, there is glaring regional disparities in the primary education. All the districts of the state are not equally advanced and well developed in the spheres of primary education. The districts are divided into dualistic nature i.e. low literacy districts and districts with more literate. This is shown in the Table 1.

Table 1. Education in Orissa – District wise

Districts	*Literacy rate 2001*	*Change over 1991*	*Teachers per School (1995-96)*	*Vacancy on Dec. 31,1998*	*Growth of Primary teachers (1995-96 to 1998-99) percent*
Group –A					
Jagatsinghpur	79.69	13.83	2.43	510	24.04
Sundargarh	65.22	12.25	2.59	403	(-) 13.19
Cuttack	76.13	10.69	2.78	744	(-) 24.07
Balasore	70.94	13.3	2.80	320	16.21
Kendrapara	77.33	13.72	3.27	288	(-) 10.34
Sonepur	64.07	21.45	2.24	123	21.23
Jajpur	72.19	14.19	2.38	276	33.25
Nayagarh	71.02	13.82	3.49	280	(-) 18.81
Ganjam	62.94	16.22	3.01	1288	(-) 0.75

Khurda	80.19	12.47	3.30	580	0.05
Puri	78.40	15.10	2.73	324	17.35
Bhadrak	74.64	14.1	2.70	289	7.22
Deogarh	60.78	16.33	2.22	26	(-) 1.30
Baragarh	64.13	16.48	2.51	153	18.73
Jharsuguda	71.47	18.83	2.59	56	5.65
Dhenkanala	70.11	15.20	2.69	693	24.33
Angul	69.40	17.87	2.47	363	29.89
Sambalpur	67.01	15.45	2.89	55	(-) 17.26
Group -B					
Gajapati	41.73	12.36	1.94	120	32.76
Kalahandi	46.20	15.12	2.24	248	5.75
Nuapada	42.29	14.47	2.79	277	5.88
Mayurbhanj	52.43	14.55	2.29	1006	24.03
Boudh	58.43	17.45	2.56	321	19.19
Nawarangpur	34.26	15.64	2.01	85	(-) 12.68
Keonjhar	59.75	15.02	2.55	370	21.71
Bolangir	54.93	16.30	2.68	367	(-) 7.96
Rayagada	35.61	9.60	2.42	577	(-) 4.00
Koraput	36.20	11.56	2.55	230	3.62
Malkangiri	31.26	11.22	1.92	168	25.77
Kandhamal	52.95	15.72	1.99	—	24.77

(***Source:*** District at a glance, 2001, Directorate of Economics & Statistics, Orissa, Education in Orissa: 1995-96, Statistics Cell, Directorate of Mass Education.)

In the above Table – 1 the districts enlisted in Group – B represents low literacy districts in Orissa, where as districts, in Group – A are comparatively highly literate districts.

GLOBALISATION AND PRIMARY EDUCATION

Globalisation has its profound impact on the educational scenario of India. Because of the adoption of new economic policy (LPG), a number of private westernized educational institutions were opened with most qualitative educational environment. On the contrary, there are schools run by the State Government with low salary to teachers (Sikhya Sahayak). Thus, there has been dualistic pattern of elementary education prevailing in our country. In the poverty stricken, tribal concentrated districts as has been observed, due to distance in the location of the schools and irregularity of teachers, there is engagement of children in various economic activities to supplement the income of the parents and the attendance percentage is very low. In this case the drop out rate in the elementary level is found as high as 60%. Parents belonging to high income groups prefer to enroll their children in the English Medium Westernized Education, so as to enable their children to compete the global job markets. Because of globalization of education, there is a frequent drop out rate among the Schedule Tribes and General students in India. This is depicted in the Table No.2.

Table 2. Dropout Rate among Scheduled Tribes and General Students in India

In percent

Classes	*Scheduled Tribes*			*General Caste Students*		
	Male	*Female*	*Total*	*Male*	*Female*	*Total*
I – V	69.94	68.73	64.53	46.74	49.69	47.93
I – VIII	76.21	81.45	78.08	59.38	68.31	65.40
I – X	84.87	89.91	86.72	72.68	79.46	75.36

Source: Education for all: The Indian, Deptt. of Education, MHRD, Govt. of India, Table –22, 1993.

It is revealed from the table – 2 that dropout rates increase when children move to higher classes. Where as the dropout rate is 64.53% upto class VI th among ST students, the percentage increases to 86.72% at

Class I – Xth level. The dropout rate is comparatively lower in case of general students as is evident from the Table – 2.

Several incentives were provided by the Government in order to provide education for all. One such instance is Mid-Day Meal Programme.

The Government provide the Mid-Day Meals in primary and upper primary schools to raise the level of literacy. But however, it has been observed that a substantial time is consumed for preparation of mid-day meal, distribution, washing and cleaning of the school. Due to the inferior quality of the food materials, small children suffer from several health hazards. Moreover, the required number of teachers are not appointed by the Government because of shrinkage of public sector investment funds in the era of globalization. Absenteeism of teachers in the classroom make the primary educational environment non competitive with the Global English Medium Schools. Further, the existing school buildings are also not so conducive to the small children to develop their mental caliber. It is feared that due to globalisation, education will favour to the students of global school (English Medium Schools). In the field of competitive examinations the students educated in normal schools would be deprived of opportunities

Thus, in the sphere of elementary education, the Govt. is facing challenges to fulfill its commitment to provide education for all. There is wide disparities not only in the flow of education to all communities but also in the sphere of maintaining equality of education. Education has been commercialized and only the affluent class of the society can have the access to such education where as the economically disadvantaged group are deprived of the benefits and hence, they lag behind.

SUGGESTIONS

Obviously, there is an imperative need to minimize the gap and eliminate the disparity,, which have been created due to globalization. Adequate infrastructure facilities should be created for better quality education. The vacancies in the field of elementary education should be filled up. Education should reach the interior pockets and inaccessible regions through television, non-formal education, mobile schools etc. Dishonest teachers and personnels engaged in imparting education should be punished and 'leakages' of fund should be checked. Govt. should confer benefits of education to all sections of the society. Left to the forces of globalization, the benefits of education will not flow automatically; hence, corrective steps should be taken by the interference of the Government.

REFERENCE:

1. - *Economic and Political Weekly,* March, 5, 2005.
2. Tripathy, S.N. and Pradhan, P (2001); *Impact of Mid Day Meal and Problems – A study,* Orissa Economic Journal, Jan – June & July – Dec, Vol. XXXIII, No. 1 &2.

10

Globalisation and Higher Education in India

Dr. Bimal Charan Swain

Sr.Lecturer in Education , Radhanath Institute of Advanced Studies in Education, Cuttack-753002 (Orissa)

GLOBALISATION: THE CONCEPT

Globalisation is a process of breaking the political, economic, social cultural, ecological, geographical and educational barriers and integrating the whole world into a "Global Village". In the globalisation process one should realize the concept like "Whole Earth is One Family". According to Knight and de Wit (1997)" Globalisation refers to the increasing flow of technology, finance, trade, knowledge, people, values and ideas across borders". International Monetary Fund (IMF) defines globalisation as "the growing economic interdependence of countries worldwide through increasing volume and variety of cross border transactions in goods and services and of international capital flows and also through the more rapid and widespread diffusion of technology". According to

Hallack (1998) "globalisation is a state of much freer trade in goods and services combined with free capital movements made at the places even unknown to its users". Hill defines globalisation as "the shift towards a more integrated and interdependent world economy. Globalisation has two main components- the globalisation of markets and the globalisation of production".

INDIAN INITIATIVES FOR GLOBALISATION

Most of global economies have chosen to move their economic systems towards the market economy and global economy. These countries include India, East European countries, Vietnam, Peru, Mexico, Brazil, Eritrea, Ethiopia, Morocoo, Chile, Spain, Cuba etc. India had observed these developments in the global economies and responded favourably to these changes in 1991 (Bolashetty, 2005).

The huge fiscal deficits, crisis in the balance of payments situation, falling foreign exchange reserves and conditions imposed by IMF led to the announcement of the New Economic Policy by the Govt. of India in July, 1991.

The New Economic Policy resulted in radical change in the structure and direction of Indian economy. The direction tends towards the market economy and globalisation of the country.

NEW ECONOMIC POLICY AND GLOBALISATION

The seeds of globalisation were shown in 1980 by granting concessions for inflow of foreign capital, allowing MNCS to enter crucial sectors, liberalizing the provisions of Foreign Exchange Regulation Act (FERA), acceleration of import liberalization process, and the downward adjustment of exchange rate of Rupee.

However, the real thrust of globalisation process has been provided in the New Economic Policy in July 1991, at the behest of the IMF and IBRD (Popularly known as World Bank).

IMF and IBRD indicated the process of globalisation in India with the following three components:

1. Cutting down the fiscal deficits and the growth rate of money supply to achieve economic stabilization.
2. Liberalizing the domestic economy by releasing the restrictions on production, investment, prices and by increasing the role of market economy, guiding and deciding resource allocation.
3. Relaxing the restrictions on external sector. These measures include: international flow of goods, services, technology and capital.

HIGHER EDUCATION IN INDIA IN POST-INDEPENDENCE PERIOD

India has the second largest higher education system in the world comprising more than 307 universities, about 15,343 colleges, some 4,36,246 teachers at the tertiary level and 192,27,833 students. The number of university level institutions has increased from 18 in 1947 to 307 by the end of 2004. At present, there is only one college for 11,000 students and one university over 4.7 lakh of students in the age group (17-23), which means that only 6.0 percent of the eligible age group is getting the benefit of higher education. But it is 100 percent in Canada, 81 in USA, 52 in France, 19 in Thailand, 14 in Mexico, 12 in Brazil and 41 percent in Argentina. Thus, It is essential to expand our higher education upto 20 percent of those who are eligible to receive Post Graduate and Graduate education in our country. The discipline wise enrolments says that in the science stream there is 19.7 percent as against 42.7 percent in arts faculty and 20.7 percent into commerce including management.

In the 10th Five Year Plan only 2.9 percent of plan outlay is allocated for education. It is also interesting to know that 68,000 Indian students went to America for higher education during 2003, where as only 7791 foreign students were coming over to India for higher education during the same period.

There is a wide disparity in quality provided to different citizens of our country. 75% of Indian children go through an educational programme of poor quality provided by colleges and universities, while 25% benefit from a small number of quality educational institutions. It is mainly because the resources and the finance provided by our state and central government are inadequate. The share of higher education in the union budget's total provision for education has fallen from 28.19% in 1990-91 to 17.7% in 2003-04. Allocation for education in the first five year plan was 7.2% of the total outlay. In the 10th Five year Plan, it has further come down to 2.9%.

Academic and administrative problems faced by the educational institutions are further compounded by government control. There is also political interference in educational institutions. The syllabus of majority of the universities reveal academic backwardness. The subjects are neither job-oriented nor life oriented. Indian universities have a significant large student to faculty ratio, when compared to global counterparts. Indian educational institutions also provide little interaction with industry.

GLOBAL VILLAGE AND EDUCATION

The changed scenario is marked by the phenomenon of "Global Village". Through efficient modes of communication, distance have reduced; world is now like a global village and continuous international interaction has become an essential component of human survival. There is a process of global and cultural unification. Revolutions in the scientific and technological fields and cybernetic and electronic information transaction are sweeping the world. The institutional education is becoming an obscure one. We are forced to face certain challenges to higher education in India. We are challenged with changes that are taking place in the world at large. Over the last twenty years, a new paradigm of the function of higher education in society has emerged (Arasu, 2005).

ENGLISH AS INTERNATIONAL COMMUNICATION

English is going to acquire the status of an international language. This has serious implications for India, because such a situation will place the product of private English medium schools at an advantageous position as compared to others.

USE OF EDUCATIONAL TECHNOLOGY

The wide use of educational technology in higher education has expanded access and spawned new ways of teaching and learning. Over the next decade, use of electronic educational technology is going to cause an increased number of institutions to offer distance learning and with much higher number of students enrolled.

HIGHER EDUCATION AND DEVELOPMENT

The development of higher education is correlated with the economic development. That is why US and

Singapore have moved their higher education system from the margins of societal concern to a core status of central importance to their societies and economics so that their quality workforce are able to compete in the world markets. Therefore, the first task that India should undertake is to expand higher education system in a planned way as to cover as large a portion of the eligible age group as possible.

PRIVATIZATION OF HIGHER EDUCATION

In the Asia-pacific region, privatization is seen as a means to increase access to higher education. This seems to be the trend in many countries. China had nearly doubled its higher education institutions since 1999 and there are already more than 1000 min ban (people run) institutions in China. In Japan private higher education accounts for 77% of the higher education in the country. In Phillipines, among the total of 1353 higher education institutions, 1189 are private institutions, which educate 70% of the students in higher education (Stella and Gananam, 2003).

Over and above, the demand for the market economy all over the world is increasingly compelling the universities and other academic institutions to introduce skill oriented courses, which require higher investment, but fetch smaller social benefits. This situation has lead to increased privatization of higher education. The Ambani-Birla report rightly stated, "A Private Universities Bill should be legislated to encourage the establishment of new private universities, a redefinition of Governments role in higher education would call for a major privatization of university education system in India" (Chauhan, 2002). States like Chhatisgarh, Uttaranchal, Tripura and Sikkim have already passed private universities bills and other states like Rajasthan, Himachal Pradesh and Pubjab are in the process of coming up with legislatures for establishment of private universities.

There is a strong argument in favour of private participation in higher education. User payments improve quality of education. When students pay directly they need to become actively involved to ensure that they receive the benefits in return.

SUGGESTIONS FOR GLOBALISATION OF INDIAN HIGHER EDUCATION

- The universities and other academic institutions need to improve their infrastructure in the form of good lecture halls, well-equipped laboratories, adequate library resources, facilities for sports, recreation facilities and hostel facilities.
- For attracting foreign students there is a need to simplify, the existing legal framework, procedures relating to registration, entry test requirement, issue of No Objection Certificate and also issue and extension of visa.
- The teacher student ratio in Indian Universities has to be reduced by recruiting more faculties. The faculties should be qualified and talented.
- The procedure for granting admission to foreign students must be simplified.
- The syllabus in different universities should be upgraded or modified in keeping with the global trends and in line with requirement of the global industry.
- Indian educational institutions should give due attention on enhancement of skills and up gradation of knowledge in order to match the human resource to the need of the new

international scenario where employment opportunities can be created.

- Universities should arrange industry friendly education that helps students to get jobs in the industry.
- Institutions need to raise funds through immovable ways, like live industry projects and obtaining funds from the industry.
- In the globalisation era all universities and educational institutions should manage their website with updating. The website should provide the main features of the institute or university, programmes available, procedure for admission, fees and scholarships available, course syllabus, faculty profiles, past results and placement details of old students.
- Global education is a two way process and it is essential that Indian universities and institutions, should develop networks with foreign universities in both the developed and developing countries.

REFERENCES

1. Arasu, J.G.V. (2005). *"Impact of Globalisation and WTO on Higher Education in India"*, ***University News***, Vol. 43, No.32, pp. 17-22.
2. Awasthi, O.N.(2002). *"Indian Education System in the Global Context"*, ***Journal of Indian Education***, Vol.28, No.1, pp. 85-100.
3. Bhalla, V. (2002*). "International Students in India, (Data for 1990-91 to 2000-01"*, in K.B. Power (Ed.) ***International of Higher Education.*** New Delhi: Association of Indian Universities, pp. 85-94.
4. Bolashetty, S.S. (2005). *"Trade in Indian Higher Education Service Sector: Implications of WTO's GATS"*,***University News***, Vol. 43,No.36, pp. 8.
5. Bolashetty, S.S. (2005). *"Trade in Indian Higher Education*

Service Sector: Implications of WTO's GATS", ***University News***, Vol. 43, No. 38, pp.6- 14.

6. Chauhan, C.P.S. (2002). *"Higher Education in India: Challenges of Global Trends"*, University News, Vol. 40, No.17, p.4.
7. Singh, R. (2005). *"Privatization of Higher Education the Era of Globalization"*, ***University News,*** Vol. 43, No.34, pp.9-11.
8. Stella, A. and Gananam, A. (2003). *"Quality Assurance Across National Boundaries: National Context and International Developments"*, ***University News,*** Vol. 41. No.11, p. -4.
9. Tilak, J.B.J. (1999). *"Privatization of Higher Education"*, ***Prospectus,*** Vol.21, No.2.
10. World Bank (1994). *Higher Education: The Lessons of Experience.* Washington: The World Bank.

11

Impact of Globalisation on Higher Education in India

Dr. Rajalakshmi Das
Sr. Lecturer in Education,
Radhanath Institute of Advanced
Studies in Education, Cuttack

Globalisation is the emerging reality of the 21st century. To-day Globalisation is the trend not only in economic, commercial and technological fields, but also in education. Globalisation refers to a package of economic reforms that include liberalization, marketisation and decentralization. Globalisation indicates 'interconnectivity' of technologies. These technologies have rapidly made the world a 'global village'. Nations, organisations, individuals, business and commercial corporations are integrated by globalisation. The global era has immense implications for education. Globalisation make education interactive, self-actualizing discovery, enjoyable and self awarding.

GLOBALISATION: THE CONCEPT

Globalisation is a process of breaking the political, economic, social, cultural, ecological, geographical and educational barriers and integrating the whole world into a 'Global Village'.

Jacques Hallack (1998) views 'globalisation' as a "state of much freer trade in goods and services combined with free capital movements made at the places even unknown to its users." These changes led to the transition of international trade to global economy and with global economy becoming supra-national, it entails varied changes. From this economic expansionist goals of some nations/states/ corporations, there arose a phenomenon of globalisation.

Stiglitz (2002) defiines globalisation as " removal of barriers to free trade and the closer integration of national economies. In other words globalisation refers to the integration of different economies of the world through trade, investment and migration of people.

According to Rangarajan (2003) "globalisation means integration of economies and societies through cross country flow of information, ideas, technology, goods, services, capital, finance and people". Globalisation in education refers to integrating an international dimension into teaching, learning and service functions of the institution.

INDIAN INITIATIVES FOR GLOBALISATION

The New Economic Policy

Most of the economies of the world have chosen to move their economic systems towards the market economy. The huge fiscal deficits, crisis in the balance of payments situation, falling foreign exchange reserves and conditions imposed by IMF led to the announcement of the New Economic Policy by the Government of India in July 1991. The New Economic Policy resulted in radical change in the structure and direction of Indian economy. The direction tends towards market economy and globalisation of the country. The objectives of New Economic Policy are;

- to obtain higher economic growth rate
- to reduce the annual rate of inflation
- to relieve the economy from critical balance of payments disequilibrium and rebuild foreign exchange reserves.

Government of India took drastic policy decisions in order to achieve these objectives.

Present Scenario of Higher Education in India

Higher Education in any society is of vital importance in the whole education system. Higher education throughout the world is in crisis. The draft proposal on higher education for 21st century envisages the quality of higher education as a multi-dimensional concept and institutions of higher learning must play a role in identifying and addressing the issues that affect the well being of communities, nations and global society. The Report - "Higher Education in Developing Countries: Peril and Promise" (2000) presented a powerful message: Higher Education is no longer a luxury, it is essential for survival."

The first three universities being set up in 1857 under the British rule were Calcutta, Bombay and Madras. By 1947 there were 18 universities in India and the total number of student strength was less than 2 lakh. After independence, there has been a phenomenal quantitative growth in higher education in India. India has earned the distinction of having the world's third largest system after USA and China. According to the Annual Report of the UGC, the total university level institutions were 342. There were 17,625 affiliated colleges. The number of students enrolled in higher education was 104.81 lakh as on 31st March, 2005. The unprecedented increase in numbers coupled with unmatched increase in infrastructure has led to dilution in standards, quality and excellence.

There is a wide disparity in quality provided to different citizens of our country. 75% of children in India go through an education programme of poor quality provided by colleges and universities, while 25% benefit from a small number of quality educational institutions. It is mainly because of the resources and the finance provided by the State and Central government are inadequate. The share of higher education in the Union budget's total provision for education has fallen from 28.19% in 1990-91 to 17.7% in 2003-04. Allocation for education in the First Five Year Plan was 7.2% of the total outlay. In the Tenth Five-Year Plan, it has further comedown to 2.9%.

The documents on Development of Higher Education in India (1978) and the Challenge of Education (1985) have rightly acknowledged of the fact that " if the present system is allowed to continue, the chasms of economic disabilities, regional imbalances and social injustices will widen further, resulting in building up of disintegrative tensions".

GLOBALISATION IN HIGHER EDUCATION

Globalisation is an inseparable reality. In education, it is visible in the form of increased flow of students from one country to another in search of higher, better or cheaper learning opportunities.

Through internationalization of education:

- Students get access to the latest knowledge and advancements in their chosen fields.
- Students become cultural ambassadors, enhancing the image of their country abroad.
- Students get first hand exposure to the culture and society of other countries by increasing international understanding.
- Institutions and countries attract foreign students get sizable economic benefits.

This process of globalisation in the field of higher education has now received a great boost with the emergence of the General Agreement on Trade in Services (GATS) regime. The General Agreement on Trade in Services (GATS) 2006 is an agreement between the countries who are signatories to WTO. The GATS aims to cover services of international trade in terms of equality with commodity trade.

Education is one of the 12 services covered under GATS. Marketing 'education' is a profitable proposition with very great potentials and possibilities. Education must possesses inbuilt 'quality', "seleable skills" competing with the best of the world need to be nurtured. Globalisation has been accelerated due to the energetic efforts of World Trade Organisation (WTO), which was established in 1995. WTO's classification list (W/120) divides educational services into five parts – Primary Education Services, Secondary Education Services, Higher Education Services, Adult Education and Other Education services. Education is included in 12 classified sectors covering 161 services, GATS extends to all countries whose educational systems are not provided by the government only. The educational systems of all the countries of the world are to be opened up as per GATS mandate.

GLOBALISATION AND INTERNATIONAL TRADE IN EDUCATION

International trade in education under the globalisation scenario initiated by the WTO is likely to take place through four modes:

1. International Distance Education Mode.
2. Inter-institutional Collaboration of two countries.
3. Institutional presence directly or through a system of franchise, and
4. Trans-national mobility of students.

79,736 Indian students had gone abroad to different countries for study during 2003-04. Only 7,791 students had come to India for study from various countries in 2000-01 (UNESCO). India's international trade as perceived from mobility from and to India clearly indicates that it is facing an unfavourable situation in the balance of trade.

Imbalance in international trade in education is due to the inability of quality institution to provide avenues of higher education, irrelevant curriculum and methods of teaching, unattractive terms and conditions of services to teachers of various grades etc.

In 2000AD, India's rank in international education index was 141 among 173 countries. Its human development index was 127 among 175 countries. India's 'educational health' is not at all satisfactory. Most of the institutions are substandard. It needs relevant quality higher education.

IMPACT OF GLOBALISATION ON HIGHER EDUCATION IN INDIA

The global era has immense implications for

education with the following thrusts:

- Demands on students and teachers to develop global consciousness and global concerns;
- Necessity to arrive at the 'frontiers of knowledge' as rapidly as possible by closing existing gaps;
- Emphasis on the development of communication skills with increasing mastery over information technology;
- Development of a global civilization and the necessity to share values that can sustain humanity in the global era; and
- Challenges to equity and opportunities for diversity.

The followings are the impact of globalisation on higher education:

The impact of globalisation in education are web based learning, use of internet in learning and research, international visit, international exchange programmes, international partnership in teaching and learning at the group, class and individual levels, interactions and sharing through video conferencing across countries, communities, institutions and individuals.

ENGLISH AS INTERNATIONAL COMMUNICATION

The process of globalisation of knowledge market education has given English Language a status of 'Lingua Franca' of international communication, because it has made dissemination of information easier and quicker especially when used with computers and internet. English is going to acquire the status of an international language.

DISTANCE EDUCATION AND GLOBAL DELIVERY OF EDUCATIONAL SERVICES

Another aspect of recent developments in electronic educational technology is the burgeoning interest in global delivery of educational services. There would be a growing trend of international student mobility. With electronic delivery methods, learning need not occur at the same time or place as instruction. With international study, learning occurs at a different time and place and the sponsoring institution has limited control over the circumstances in which it takes place.

Distance Education in recent times is accepted as an alternative channel to democratize education all over the world. Distance education facilitates, self-paced learning and flexibility in terms of entry and exist. It also allows flexibilities in time, pace, and place of learning. Distance education has been meeting the ever growing demand of higher education as the scope of expansion of the formal system of higher education is limited.

IMPACT ON TEACHING

Globalisation has its impact on teaching. Through globalisation, multiple sources of teaching are available. Teaching can become world-class. Through participation in international development and research programmes, teachers can achieve global out look. Their teaching can become networked teaching. A new professional culture can grow and they can share professional practice and research (Panneerselvam, 2004).

CURRICULUM

Curriculum acquires a new scene in globalisation.

The curriculum content pools up the world class materials and designs for the teaching and learning process and maximizing the global relevance and exposure to the future development of individuals and the society. The curriculum becomes relevant to globalisation of technology, economic, social, political, culture development and improvement in learning process.

USE OF ELECTRONIC EDUCATIONAL TECHNOLOGY

Globalisation will definitely make education interactive, self-actualizing discovery, enjoyable, and self-awarding. The wide use of educational technology in higher education has expanded access and spawned new ways of teaching and learning. Use of electronic educational technology is going to cause an increased number of institutions to offer distance learning and with much higher number of students enrolled. There will be a greater variety of learning sites and modes. There will be an increasing number of students who would seek recognition for distance based courses to fit in a greater diversity of study objectives of individual students (Arasu, 2005).

FINANCIAL CRISIS

According to the recent reports of UNESCO and the World Bank, social and private returns of higher education are less than those of primary and secondary education. It is estimated that social return of primary education is 25% while that of higher education is 1%. This has led to the thinking that the returns of higher education are largely personal and therefore, subsidy on this should be reduced. In reality many of the state universities are facing difficulty even in the payment of the salary bills of its employees including teachers.

INTERNATIONAL INFLUENCES IN INDIAN HIGHER EDUCATION

The impact of British Higher education is felt not only in basic structure of Indian Higher Education – the system of examination, structure of post secondary education, scheme of universities and affiliating colleges but also in the range of colonial era institutions that are still among the most elite in India today. In post independence era, the Indian Institutes of Technology, consciously patterned after the Massachusetts Institute of Technology in the U.S. received substantial overseas help right from the outset. The Indian Institutes of Management established similar international links: IIM Ahmedabad maintains strong connections with the Harvard Business School. The recent innovation in Indian Higher Education, the Indira Gandhi National Open University, (IGNOU)* drew heavily on the UK experience with distance education and Open University concept.

ADVANTAGES OF GLOBALISATION

The advantages of globalisation as given by Bolashetty (2005) are:

- Free flow of capital and increase in the total capital employed.
- Free flow of technology
- Increase in industrialization
- Spread of production facilities through out the globe.
- Balanced development of world economies.
- Increase in production and consumption.
- National sovereignty at stake.
- Commodities at lower price with high quality.

- Cultural exchange and demand for a variety of products.
- Increase in jobs and income.
- Higher standards of living.
- Balanced human development.
- Increase in welfare and prosperity (Bolashetty, 2005)

DISADVANTAGES

The disadvantages of globalisation are:

- Globalisation kills domestic business
- Exploits human resource
- Leads to unemployment and underemployment
- Decline in demand for domestic products.
- Decline in income
- Widening gap between rich and poor.
- Transfer of natural resources
- Leads to commercial and political colonialism (Bolashetty, 2005)

To conclude, meaningful and responsible strategies including flexible and pragmatic education policies would strengthen the basis of global education and promise for man the realization of a dream to bring all learners and teachers under one umbrella.

REFERENCES

1. Arasu, J.G.V. (2005). "*Impact of Globalisation and WTO on Higher Education in India*" ***University News***, Vol. 43, No.32.
2. Bolashetty, S.S. (2005). "*Trade in India Higher Education Service Sector: Implications of WTO's GATS*", ***University News***, Vol. 43, NO.36.
3. Hallack, J. (1998). "*Education and Globalisation*", I.I.E.P. ***News Letter.***

4. Panneerselvam, S.K. (2004). *"Impact of Globalisation on Human Development and Education in the 21st Century"*, ***University News***, Vol. 42, No.21.
5. Rangarajan, C. (2003), *"Globalisation and Its Impact"* in ***Indian Economy Since Independence,*** New Delhi: Academic Foundation, p.729.
6. Stiglitz, J. (2002). *"Globalisation and its Discontents"*, ***Penguin,*** p. IX

12

Privatisation of Higher Education in the Globalised Era

Dr. Surekha Sundari Swain

Programme Co-ordinator, NSS, Utkal University,
Vani Vihar,Bhubaneswar (Orissa)

In the era of globalisation, education has been considered as a lucrative commodity, under General Agreement on Trade in Services (GATS). Education has been treated as an international trading commodity due to adoption of liberalized economy and efforts of WTO and World Bank. Adoption of GATS in education has resulted in two major and immediate consequences - 1) Privatisation of higher education and 2) international trading or globalisation of higher education. The international trading of higher education is also carried out by private bodies/ institutions instead of government institutions. Due to restrictions and financial problems the developing countries are unable to invest high in higher education as a result the private investment and participation increased which made higher education a real commodity and commercial venture. During the 1970's and 80's the state structure of higher education was blocked due to pressure and the flood gates were opened for privatization of higher education. The state's control on higher education has loosened. Higher education has been affordable to the smaller group who has the capacity to afford.

PRIVATISATION

Privatisation refers to the shifting of activities, assets and responsibilities from the government to private sector. This also includes a wide range of public private partnership, creation of federal corporations, quasi government organizations, and government sponsored activities. Also, privatization is often thought of as' liberalization- where agents are freed from government regulations or as 'marketisation'- where new markets are created as alternatives to government services or state allocation systems (Levin, 2001). Privatisation is the act of reducing the role of government or increasing the role of the private sector, with production and finance as the distinguishing characteristics. (De Angelo & Cohen, 2000). Privatization calls for substantially trimming the scope and breadth of government services, replacing them with private or other non-government operators (Rehfuss, 1995). The controversy in privatization of higher education is mainly based on two issues i.e. 'Trading of Education' or 'Commercialization of Education' and the 'higher goal of education'.

According to the first group of thinkers on trading of education "The supply of education should be according to the individual and market needs. There should be free access to market players. The education is considered as a 'product' and the students as 'consumers'. There should be free competition in the market place. The market players should be able to select a product, enter the market for profit. If the product is not in demand, they should be able to drop it or exit the market' (Chaturvedi, S. 2005).

The second group of thinkers on "Role of Education" opine that History of Education is meant for greater objective of social development, good citizenship, advancement of general well-being and economic competitiveness of societies. Education is a means of gaining and sharing knowledge and cultural heritage of a society. Education is an instrument of social change and social control. Hence education should not be only an economic tradable commodity. If this type of privatization continues, Higher Education would be so costly that it will be beyond the reach of the large deserving but economically and socially deprived groups. Commercialization and privatization of higher education would go against the constitutional obligation of providing equal opportunities of education to all at different levels. Leaving educational decisions on the market forces would result in increased inequalities in the distribution of human capital, which results in distribution of income. UNDP (1990) opines that higher education not only raises productivity and incomes but also facilitates the inter cost mobility thus reducing inequalities in income and wealth, it acts as 'social lift agent'. Tilak (1991) described that privatization and marketisation of higher education will ultimately lead to commercialization, because the private bodies invest in higher education with a profit motive and with a motive of social development or advancement. The report, on "Higher Education in Developing Countries: Peril and Promise", published in 2000, suggested that: Higher Education is no longer a luxury; it is essential for survival. The report of the

Task Force of UNESCO and World Bank on Higher Education and Society suggested that the world is passing through a "knowledge revolution" yet the four major principles which govern the higher education system i.e. quality assurance, access, equity and accountability continue to be the guiding forces while planning for higher education.

GLOBALISATION OF HIGHER EDUCATION

Today no nation of the world can remain in isolation from the rest of the world, because the world of to-day has shrunk into the form of a "Global Village". (Magotra, 2007) As India is a signatory in the General Agreement on Trade in Services (GATS) and member of the World Trade Organisation (WTO), it is in favour of the inter nationalization of higher education. In the year 2000, the United States representative to the WTO proposed the addition of higher education services to GATS, with United States holding the largest market share including recruitment of international students, establishment of university campuses abroad, franchised provision and online learning. The following five education sectors are covered under GATS: primary education, secondary education, Higher Education (including post secondary technical and vocational education services), adult education and other education (e.g. testing and certification). There are several ways and modes of delivery of education services.

- Cross border supply (e.g. distance education)
- Consumption abroad (e.g. students studying abroad).
- Commercial presence (e.g. Campus abroad).
- Presence of natural persons from supplying country in consuming country (e.g. faculty

teaching abroad).

Government can make commitments for one area, several, all sectors, or one of them (Mannivannan, 2004). Globalisation refers to access of knowledge across boarders. It means actual presence of an educational service provider of a country in another country and giving a foreign degree to the students. Cross border supply includes courses through distance education, on line courses through internet, educational testing services and educational materials that are provided overseas. It includes sale of paperback editions of books and sale of educational CDs.

"AIU has recently published data relating to number of foreign students studying in India. A cursery look at the advertisements published by the education service providers in India indicate how the GATS provisions are helping the free trade in education particularly higher education.

As of now, it is not favourable to India as the number of foreign students educating in India has come down substantially from around 8000 to 4000 during 1995-2000. It is reported that international student mobility in OECD countries during the last 20 years is doubled. They receive around 85% of the world foreign students. Export revenue in 1999 was amounted to $ 33 billion not less than the income on financial services. The trend shows that the developing countries will not be benefited by the free trade in education services. Further, the presence of international traders in India has attracted the rich clients towards these institutes robbing off this opportunity to the best private providers with Indian flag. Realizing the dangers of GATS provisions for higher education, the international organizations representing 5500 associations signed a declaration in 2002 at Porto Alegre opposing the introduction of GATS. Interestingly the signatories include university presidents from Latin American, American and third world educational organizations. The fear expressed by these organizations is that the advanced countries will hegemonise higher education that keeps the identity of a nation. Higher education is not just an extension of school education. It is an important and major activity in life span of an individual that will help to mould the destiny of a nation. You may loose your economy; you may also perish as individuals, but if your education is in your hands, you can rebuild all that is lost. This is proved after the II World War. Japan, Germany and even Soviet Union could rebuild their economies and societies because they have their 'own' education system. The white paper presented by the Tony Blair government in UK in January 2003 clearly demonstrates that if a country needs its identity and keeps pace with progress of others, the state has no alternative except to invest in education. Of course, allow the private investment also to supplement the state. But all the programmes must be monitored, regulated and standardized by the state keeping in view its ethos, resources and possibilities (Chalam, 2004).

FEAR OF COMMERCIALIZATION

Privatisation and Commercialization are the two sides of the same coin. No private individual or group can set up educational institutions unless some profit making motive is involved. Commercialization of higher education may provide quality education and excellence, but the government should enforce rules to standardize fee structure and regulate the process of payment of salaries to teachers. It is experienced that the newly established private institutions are charging high capitation fees for admission and not paying full salaries to the teachers. Sometimes below standard teachers are also recruited and there is no job security of the teachers. In order to curb commercialization, institutions will have to be graded for their quality performance and product. But the fundamental research in the subjects like literature, philosophy and history that promote the culture of the country will suffer. Hence there should be a uniform system of education in the country with a regulatory body, which must be autonomous and non discriminatory in nature. Vocationalisation and fundamental research should be given greater emphasis.

MERITS AND DEMERITS OF PRIVATISATION

Merits

Roger Geiger (1986) has described the merits and demerits of privatization that have got relevance to Indian higher education which are as follows:-

Privatisation of higher education provides cultural pluralisation by providing new opportunities and access to formerly excluded population. There is involvement and contribution of private bodies by mobilizing private resources to higher education to increase the quality. They are able to mobilize human resources and also are able to bring the resources of private philanthropy to higher education. In the context of financial crunch by the government, the privatization can enhance the future well-being of higher education. It is one of the superior ways of organizing the task of higher education; the public sector should also develop side by side.

Demerits

Privatisation can misuse to exploit the gullible

and lead to commercialization. They may also sell certificates of degrees and diplomas. There are many examples of Mushroom growth of private colleges without required infrastructure and teaching staff in Madhya Pradesh, Chhatishgarh and U.P. As reported by Sant (2004), during 2003, 78 private universities have come up in Chhatishgarh some of which exists in pen and paper and some have reported to have campuses in the adjourning states like Orissa and Andhra Pradesh.

Privatisation of higher education will perpetuate inequalities in the system. Higher education, the 'public' or the 'Quasi Public Good' will turn out to be a luxury good and the middle and upper middle class people will not be able to afford it. It will become a monopoly of the rich. The private universities and institutions will not merely cover their cost, but also make huge 'quick profits' which are not necessarily reinvested in education (Kaul, 1993). Walford (1990) finds that privatization at higher level contributes to persistence of socio economic inequalities in the society, providing elitist bias in education. Private institutions are profit oriented, with little consideration for national manpower needs, which may cause serious imbalance in the manpower in the economy.

SUGGESTIONS

Privatization has already entered the Indian market in the field of professional and technical education like Medical, Engineering, IT, Computer Education, Management Education, Teacher Education, Mass Communication and Journalism etc. It cannot be stopped in the era of liberalization and globalization. But some guiding principles and some check and balance should be there for effective privatization to curb commercialization. Aggarwal and Sharma (2004) have suggested the following strategies for effective privatization.

1. The National level regulating bodies like UGC, AICTE, NCTE and the like should give recognition to privately managed institutions to ensure quality and standards in education.
2. The Govt. should exercise some control over the standards of these private institutions.
3. Educational decisions should not be left on the market forces since it may result in increased inequalities in distribution of human capital and therefore, in the distribution of income. To over come this, a three tier system of fee structure should be adopted viz:
   (a) Full recovery of the cost of education from the persons having paying capacity – i.e. the elites.
   (b) Facilities of loan with low interest rate to meritorious students who cannot pay for their education.
   (c) Financial incentives like free education, subsidization and scholarships to deprived and financially weaker meritorious students.
4. The merit should be the primary consideration for admission, not the money.
5. Selection of faculty should be based on academic qualification, excellence and merit.
6. Student teacher ratio should be prescribed.
7. There should be proper manpower planning to maintain balance between supply and demand in every field.
8. The license permit for entry of private institutions

should be given to the dedicated individuals and association of lesser means.

9. There should be structural reforms that would allow only recognized players to operate in the market.
10. On the basis of the order of the Supreme Court a legal framework should be provided to higher education system.

CONCLUSION

Private participation in higher education is not new in India. It existed in various forms till the Britishers left this country. The Supreme Court of India has given a judicious vision of privatization and many other issues requiring interpretations of the provisions of the constitution. The Apex Court has given Gandhian touch of morality to trade in services as given by WTO and GATS in terms of profit motives in privatization. There is an urgent need to revisit the implementation of private universities Act 1995. There should be transparency and accountability in the privately managed institutions to meet the challenges of the 21st century.

REFERENCES

1. Agarwal, V. and Sharma, U.R. (2004). *"Privatisation and Commercialisation of Higher Education: Some Facts, Concerns and Suggestion,"* ***University News***, 42 (7).
2. Ambani, M. (2000). *Report on a Policy Framework for Reforms in Education, Prime Minister's Council for Trade and Industry,* New Delhi: Govt. of India.
3. Chalam N.S. (2004). *"Privatisation of Higher Education under WTO Region"*, ***University News*** 42 (7).
4. Chaturvedi, S. (2005). *"Privatisation of Higher Education: Issues and Challenges"*, ***University News***. 43(43).
5. Chauhan, C.P.S. (2004). *"Privatisation of Higher Education:*

A Socio economic Perspective", ***University News***, 42 (7).

6. Kaul, R. (1993). *Caste, Class and Education: Politics of the Capitation Fee Phenomenon in Karnataka,* New Delhi: Sage.
7. Levin, H.M. (2001). *Privatising Education, Can the Market Deliver Freedom of Choice, Productive Efficiency, Equity and Social Cohesion?* Boulder, Co West View Press.
8. Mannivannan, D.G. (2004). *"The Implication of GATS Trade in HE Services: The Indian Perspective of Private Participation,* ***University News*** 42 (07).
9. Sant, B.R. (2004). *"Private Participation in Indian Higher Education: Towards Excellence on Teaching and Learning*", ***University News*** 42 (7)
10. Tilak, J.B.G. (1999). "*Privatisation of Higher Education*", ***Prospects***, 21 (2).
11. Walford J. (1990). *Privatisation and Privilege in Education.* London: Knowledge,
12. World Bank (2002). *Constructing Knowledge Societies. New Challenges for Tertiary* .....***www.worldbank.org.***

13

Globalisation and Education

Dr. Droupadi Patel
Sr. Lecturer in Education, Radhanath Institute of Advanced Studies in Education, Cuttack

The increasing trend of liberalization, privatization and globalization has embarked upon a continuous chain of changes and challenges in education at the global level. Structural as well as functional changes have been effected in Indian education. In every aspect of education such as content, methodology, aims and objectives, values, economic relations, managerial rights etc., changes were effected during the last 10-15 years. Education is now treated as a commodity and access is given to private parties and foreign institutions to enter into education scene at different capacities, the trend seems to be for profit making through all possible means. Different private institutions have come out to start courses in high technology and fashionable areas like Information Technology, Biotechnology etc. The participation of private bodies may dramatically change the situation because a lot of money will be made by them. International Quality education may come with higher price tag. They may provide all facilities and pay huge salaries to their faculties as their fees are expected to be high. Students may go around the globe during various Semesters. They may develop world class academic programmes and have expert faculty members from different parts of the globe and may provide opportunity for our students to have quality education without leaving their hometowns or country. This situation may develop healthy competition among Universities in the world and raise the standard of our universities. Let us look at some other effects of globalization in the field of education.

- Higher education goes beyond the reach of average and poor people. Those who can afford, they only can go for higher and professional education. After completing the course they try to recoup the money they spend with compound interest resorting to all foul means. Thus education becomes less beneficial to society. It is said that the more you get educated, the more you become corrupt and non-service minded.
- The craze for foreign degrees and courses affects the popularity of Indian courses.
- Due to flourishing of all self-financing institutions and paying capacity of the students / parents, transparency is gradually lost and commercialization gets established.
- Due to mushrooming of unaided professional institutions, entry depends not on merit or competence but mostly on money power. This will decrease social obligation and service mentality.
- Due to computers and teaching machines, the human side of education and the sacredness of teaching position will get lost.

- Interestingly there are no takers of basic sciences, the mother of all technologies and for Arts and Humanities. Professional courses are preferred.
- Lack of clarity regarding privatization, lack of boldness to implement labour law reforms, down sizing bureaucratic hurdles and so on are retarding India's reform process. Lack of clarity in policies and delays can make the situation worse instead of realizing the objectives of liberalization.
- The liberalization of trade in services will lead to the domination of the service sectors of the developing countries by the multi-nationals of the industrialized countries. As a matter of fact, the developed countries already dominated the trade in services. The developing countries are not importers of services and their deficit has been ever growing.
- Although many services are labour intensive and therefore the developing countries should be expected to have an advantage here, there have been several constraints in benefiting from this advantage. These include technical, organizational, financial and legal. Moreover, immigration laws of developed countries restrict the manpower flow from the developing to developed countries. This severely limits the scope of developing countries in benefiting from their comparative advantage.
- Liberalisation occurs in the presence of inadequate or appropriate domestic regulation may only aggravate internal distortions and can have adverse social ramifications. There is a need for an integrated approach to social and economic policy making.

These are said to be the likely result of globalization. This trend may affect the future of the country as a whole. Thus our motto should be to widen the access and ensure success. Both equality and excellence are very much essential.

REFERENCES

1. Kumaran,D. (2002) : *Quality in Higher Education.* Journal of All India Association for Educational Research, Bhubaneswar.
2. Edutrack (2005): A monthly scanner of Trends in Education, Hyderabad.
3. National Policy on Education (1986) and POA (1992) published by M.H.R.D., New Delhi
4. Raman, A. (2004): *Quality Management and Quality Assurance in Higher Education.* New Frontiers in Education, International Journal of Education, New Delhi.
5. Ranga Reddy, A (2007): *Need of Entrepreneurial Universities for Creative Knowledge.* University News (Association of Indian Universities).

14

E-Learning

Dr. Sudhansu Kumar Das
Faculty of Commerce, S. G. College,
Kanikapada, Jajpur. (Orissa)

INTRODUCTION

Education has universally viewed as an essentially important vehicle for the socio-economic development of any nation and has been recognized as a distinguishing mark between a developed and an under developed country. It was indeed Swami Vivekananda, the great Indian hero and out-standing social reformer, once said, "I see before my eyes, a nation is developed in proportion as education and intelligence spread among masses". His words are really true in the present context, when the modern technology and knowledge are considered to be the true resources of the nation and not the physical resources. Keeping in view the importance of education, United Nations Organisation(UNO) has rightly recognized universalisation of education as its key Millennium Development Goal(MDG).

Education in general and higher education in particular has been emphasized as an important tool of social change by many social scientists and development agencies. In its draft resolution on

"Change and Development of Higher Education", UNESCO (1994) has strongly upheld the importance of higher education as an instrument of economic enhancement and social change. During the last few decades, the higher education system has undergone a sea change. The system has witnessed both structural and policy level changes in response to the change in the socio-economic scenario of the world, coupled with technological innovations and scientific developments.

Gone are those days when teachers and students within their formal set up were confined to classroom learning. With so many developments in the global education arena, the outdated teaching methods are replaced by modern learning aids. Explosion of knowledge and information is rapidly changing the present world from an industrial economy to knowledge economy, where the ancient belief that knowledge is wealth has assumed prominence. In a globalised knowledge economy, knowledge and information are replacing labour and capital to be the factors of production, making the economic activities knowledge based, rather than wealth based.

GLOBALISATION AND HIGHER EDUCATION IN INDIA

Globalisation is a structural change in the global economy that the entire world is witnessing since mid eighties. It aims at integrating the world economy by reducing the regional barriers and over coming the boundaries of nationality. Globalisation, liberalization and privatization have increased competitiveness in all the sectors of the economy including the education. All these have brought new challenges and opportunities for the higher education sector. Indian education system in particular is considerably influenced by the impact of globalization. India is today the third largest and fast growing economy of the world with annual economic growth of about 9 per cent. To keep pace with the economic growth and to face the cross boarder competitions, the nation needs huge quality manpower.

However India is far behind than the other developed, developing and neighbouring countries, so far as achievements in education is concerned. According to 2001 Census, literacy rate of the country is estimated to be only 64.84 per cent. Enrollment of student to primary education is 70 per cent, 40 per cent in secondary education and alarmingly low of only 11 per cent in higher education. In higher education front, the number of universities in India is estimated to be 369 against 1500 in China. The country is running deficit of manpower by 25 per cent in English and 45 per cent in other languages. Statistics show that, despite 57 per cent growth in the number of institutions between 2000 and 2005, the growth in enrollment in higher education is estimated to be only 20 per cent.

ICT- A BOON TO HIGHER EDUCATION

Scientific innovations and technological up gradation have become the essence of life today by maximizing welfare of the people. Information Communication Technology (ICT) is a wonderful product of scientific innovations that has revolutionized the way of modern life style and socio-economic activities. It refers to creation, gathering, processing, storage, distribution and delivery of information. Higher education being the most important segment of socio-economic activities is influenced by ICT to a great extent.

ICT has revolutionized the system of teaching,

learning and research. The entire horizon of education is coloured with the popular concepts of Internet, World Wide Web (WWW), Cyberspace, Online Learning etc. Over the world software majors and universities are gearing up with computer based learning with advanced online programmes through exercise and modules. In the next decade an university may mean your study room and a computer a data link. Growing use of IT has brought a significant change in the structure of higher education, making teaching and learning more easy and efficient.

Internet is a worldwide, self-guided network connecting thousands of sub networks, millions of computers and the people of wide range of informations. All the stakeholders of education including the teachers, students, researchers, administrators and policy makers are benefited by their access to information through Internet, which is an important indicator of Human Development Index (HDI). The rapid and unforeseen proliferation of Internet through developed world has left its impact on the developing world including India.

ICT AND INDIAN HIGHER EDUCATION SYSTEM

India is not a new entrant so far as the use of ICT is concerned. The country has taken the lead in distance education more than two decades ago. The beginning was made during mid seventies with Satellite Instruction Television Experiment (SITE). India has a unique opportunity to be global leader in the field of information and technology. It is said that the 21st century will be of the Asian countries due to growing importance of ICT. There are many successful stories regarding use of ICT in the field of education. One of these is the "Laptop School", a one-month course of

Tara Akhaya Programme active in the state of Bihar, U.P, Haryana, Himachal Pradesh. This is a literacy mission by the Sehgal Foundation started in May 05, to spread primary education in the remote and educationally backward regions. Similarly, Indian Institute of Technology (IIT), Bangalore has taken the lead to open its lecture online to the technical colleges of the country through Edusat.

PRESENT STATUS AND FUTURE CHALLENGES:

Vastness is the unique feature of higher education system of the country. Since independence the number of universities in the country has gone up from 19 in 19 47 to 369 in 2006. There are about 15000 affiliated colleges in the country with more than 3 lakh teachers. Number of students enrolled in the higher education ranges between seven and eight millions. Despite this only 6 to 7 per cent of our youth in the age group of 18 and 23 years are enrolled in higher education. In a recent study it has been estimated that enrolment in higher education is only 8.9 per cent, which is far below than the estimated growth of 20 per cent in higher education sector in the last academic year.

So far as student enrollment in professional education in the country is concerned, the situation is alarming. Enrollment of students in faculties of engineering and medicine is estimated to be 7.5 per cent and 3.5 per cent respectively. It is only 2 per cent in agriculture and allied trade. In contrast to this, 30 per cent study engineering in Japan. A large segment (about 75 per cent) of the students in India is studying social studies, humanities and general science in formal educational institutions. The formal educational institutions in the country have failed to enrich the aspiration of the students. According to the report of the Parliament Standing Committee on Human Resources Development (2006), only 16 out of every 1000 in rural and 111 in urban sector are graduates.

On the academic front, the situation is again a matter of concern. Indian Universities are suffering from poor infrastructure, shortage of faculties, traditional method of teaching and outdated course curriculum. By the end of March 2006, there were 1988 vacancies in 16 central universities, out of which 1056 are of the post of lecturers. Again, there exist qualitative and quantitative differences between the premier professional institutions, central universities, state universities and private universities. The country has vast manpower, big proportion of youth people and a vast structure of education system. The need is to capitalize these resources.

CONCLUSION

Higher education being the important sector of the Indian Economy has witnessed the impact of liberalization and globalisation with the entry of many private and foreign players. With increasing inducement of IT in the industrial sector, generation of IT professionals is becoming a crucial factor. The country is to set up new paradigm in the field of training and development of IT professionals in addition to its formal education to generate quality manpower to meet its immediate needs. The training industry of the country is growing with public and private partnership. Apart from this MNCs and Indian companies are sponsoring fellowship and master degree programmes in IT related fields. According to N.R.Narayan Murty, former M.D of Infosys, "While the universities and institutions in the formal sector and a few private training institutes offer a good standard of learning, the graduates still need to be retained in the latest applications and methodologies.

There is a long way to go for the Indian universities and colleges to be technically upgraded in order to face the challenges arising out of developments in macro educational scenario. The colleges and schools with awareness and access to ICT will be the way to the knowledge world, which will be of immense help in generating quality and technically developed workforce. This in return will benefit the nation with the fruits of e-governance, e-commerce, tele-medicine, e-learning and in many other fields. Our dream to have a prosperous and developed nation free from hunger and poverty will be a reality when there is a perfect and objective combination of technology, innovation and education.

REFERENCES

1. Raghavan. V.P., "*Knowledge Economy: A Dual Perspective*", Kurukshetra, February 2006.
2. - IT Digest, Various Issues.
3. Reddy. A.R., "*IT in our Lives*", Yojana, November 2003.
4. - Business Standard, November 25, 2007.
5. - Economic Times, Various Issues.

15

Trends in Higher Education During Globalisation

Dr. Bijaylaxmi Das
Lecturer in Education,
Sri Jaydev College of Education and
Technology, Naharkanta, Khurda, (Orissa)

INTRODUCTION

India is one of the most ancient civilizations in the world with a rich cultural heritage. It got independence in 1947 and became republic in 1950. The country has made rapid progress in terms of social, economical and cultural development. It has a long history of its own and has a long tradition of learning. The ancient higher learning centres in India were the leading institutes in the contemporary world and attracted scholars from different countries. Takshashila (West Punjab), Purushpur (Peshwar), Vikramshila and Nalanda (Bihar), Kanchi (Madras) were the beacon lights where there were no means of communication and connectivity but they had attracted thousands of students from other neighbouring countries. Education imparts knowledge and skills and shape values and attitude in this growing competitive global world. It is vital for population control, poverty reduction, economic growth, civic order, culture and citizenship education. Generally, education helps in strengthening civil institutions, building, national capacity and good governance.

Twenty first century is considered as the knowledge era. In the knowledge economy of tomorrow, the learning organizations alone will survive. Education is becoming even more vital in the new world of information. Knowledge is rapidly replacing raw materials and labour the most critical input for survival and success. Thus education and knowledge are at the central stage of any development process. The global labour market is increasingly integrated with the highly knowledgeable and skilled corporates, executives, scientists and technologists offering high mobility and wages. No doubt, the world has materially progressed a lot and the society has also overcoming the tremendous challenges of hurdles which are created by human beings. During this day, when science and technology has influenced tremendously, the way of life of human beings with every sort of facilities and comforts, they have a gloomy picture being deprived of the benefits flowing from this advancement. The elite groups like politicians, industrialists are exploiting those groups who are deprived of such advancement in the global world. The progress and prosperity of one nation gets affected by the position and status of other countries of the world. So we should try to save the global world from all such things only through higher education. By educating the human being properly we can make this world heaven on the earth worth to live in real sense.

PRESENT SCENARIO OF HIGHER EDUCATION

The present educational system as described by WTO can be classified into five segments as primary, secondary, higher, adult and other education. Higher education is in the priority list under "public education sector". Following the principles of globalisation, the government of India has opened 'Higher education' sector for the indigenous and alien beneficiaries.

India has one of the largest "Higher Education Centres" in the world. Today with more than hundred crore population we have 247 universities and 98 deemed universities, where as Japan with its 12.7 crore population has 684 universities, USA with 27.6 crore population has 2364 universities and Germany with 8.25 crore population has 330 universities. A big gap is quite evident to come close to Japan and USA roughly where as 6000 to 9000 universities are required to be established in India. (Kale, 2006). The enrolment percentage in higher education is only six percent which shows a big difference from other countries. There are several organizations involved in the filed of higher education system in the country. They include UGC which is responsible for co-ordination, determination and maintenance of standards and release of grants.

Professional Councils are responsible for recognition of courses, promotion of professional institutions and providing grants to undergraduate programmes and various awards. The statutory professional councils are AICTE, DEC, ICAR, BCI, NCTE, RCI, PCI, INC, DCI and CCIM which are providing higher education in our country.

In terms of GDP (Pillai, 2006), the percentage of allocation of funds for higher education in India has constantly decreased from 1 percent in 1971 to 0.4

percent in 2001, where as this position of USA 6.5%, France 5.8%, Germany 4.6%, Thailand 5% and even Kenya 6.2% is much better and an eye opener.

In the UNESCO world conference on Higher Education, India presented a paper entitled, "Higher Education in India; Vision and Action." In that paper, the author quoted, "No plan for the future development of the country can be deemed to be complete which does not provide for technical and scientific training. This is an age of machine and it is only those countries which arisen to the highest pitch that will survive in the struggle that will commence when the war is over for maintaining decent standards of living for the people"

HIGHER EDUCATION IN GLOBALIZED WORLD

The beginning of the 21st century has marked separation of knowledge from information. The new form of globalization in higher education has exploited, the potential of new information and communication technologies in the field of management, industry and business for academic exchange in the world.

The globalisation phenomenon changed the world in providing the innovative forms of education computer and communication technologies. Internet have accelerated the process of education, easy for the students to study and learn outside their country. Today, no nation of the world can remain isolated from the rest of the world due to the form of "global village". Higher education is now being considered as a commodity to be bought and sold. The report, higher education in developing countries: peril and promise, published in 2000, presented a powerful message; "Higher education is no longer a luxury; it is essential for survival" thus, renewal of higher education is essential for the whole society to be able to ensure its intellectual independence, create knowledge and educate and train responsible enlightened citizens and qualified specialists without whom no nation can progress economically, socially, culturally and politically (UGC, Vision and strategy for 10th five year plan, part –I).

Indians have made their presence felt in the field of science, humanities, economic politics and others too. They have acted, as backbone in many global science and technology revolutions but this is also a major crisis for us as they are pulled towards the developed countries where they have got the higher power and better economic benefit. So globalisation is not meant for higher education only but for the betterment of income among the countries and within the countries. Because, in this new society only 'fittest' who are capable of being 'adoptive', adaptive and adept would survive. Thus, it is the duty of every educated and enlightened member of India that he **should** not allow any body whosoever high and mighty to exploit students or reaching communities for their personal benefits. Thus the Indian citizens should be aware of the quality of education of developed economy to run their nation in a progressive way. In the present context higher education not only provides high skills for labour market but also the learning and training required for different professionals such as teachers, doctors, engineers, civil servants etc. These trained individuals in their own field drive local economies which in turn affect government and society. In order to fulfil their educational functions the purpose of higher education needs to be changed. Institutions are no longer transformed the preservation of authorized knowledge and organized discipline but to respond towards educational needs particularly in the context of globalization and a borderless market.

In India 2020: A vision for new Millenium, Dr. APJ Abdul Kalam with Dr. Y.S. Ranjan (1998) have discussed the potential of India to be a developed nation. It is also mentioned that transmission is possible only by exploiting one billion of people as resource. The billion people are real wealth of the nation. It is pertinent to mention that economic growth theories have emphasized the role of human capital as the key for economic growth and development (Tripathy, 2004). The Human Development Report published in 1990 opened with the words, " The real wealth of a nation is its people. " Thus the people should be educated and collect experiences for their nation. The quality and standard of education can provide better higher education to the people for the advancement of the country. Higher Education empowers the individual to acquire skills and competencies for achieving their social goals.

MEASURES FOR HIGHER EDUCATION

Higher education system in India, however, is experiencing problems in relation to size, access, equity, relevance, quality and research crunch. Some of the measures should be taken in higher education for the 21st century.

1. The share of higher education in the total expenditure on education of the union government has declined from 7.2% in first five year plan to 2.9% in 10th five year plan. Thus, the budget should be increased for providing quality education in the university level.
2. To recruit competent teachers and expose them periodically for advance training in their areas of

specialization.

3. Creating conditions in which teachers have the time to teach and the ability to teach well.
4. Equip our teachers more seriously to be able to help students from different background to achieve excellence.
5. Research in various disciplines has developed in such an extent that it should be investigated in new areas with new directions for the quality research. Sufficient books, journals, equipments and human resources should be provided.
6. Policies should be finalized by the government relating to the promotion of Indian education abroad.
7. The government should advise Indian embassies and High commissioners abroad to play a protective role in providing information regarding the facilities available in higher education in India.
8. There is now to adopt an open door policy for self financing students.
9. The government should consider establishing a financial mechanism for international education such as a possible international educational development bank.
10. The government should set up a mechanism for monitoring the standard of education that is imparted by foreign universities.
11. Institution should raise the fee level in such a way that at least 20% of the annual recurring cost per student is covered from the students in the form of fees and from other sources. The institutions should also raise resources from other internal and external sources by diversifying their activities into different fields.

CONCLUSION

While some reforms are necessary to improve the efficiency of higher education, some attempts should be taken to achieve the well cherished higher education Emphasis is laid on financial efficiency, measured in terms of resource generation in stead of academic excellence. There is a need to balance the main functions of higher education and resource needs of the system. The basic, characteristics of higher education, such as the 'public' good nature of higher education and social value of higher education in one hand and the needs of the new globalised Indian economy on the other should be kept in mind while formulating policies for the development of higher education. The authorities to regulate higher education must remain in the hands of competent bodies and ensure academic excellence, encouragement, stop malpractices, stop charging capitation fee, stop profiteering. If the Indian citizens do not become aware of their quality of education, the nation will suffer a lot and the economy and good governance shall be destroyed. The education committees who are the builders of the nation should awaken the public for future globalised world.

Our Ex-president Hon'ble Dr. APJ Abdul Kalam has rightly said, " A developed India by 2020 or even earlier is not a dream. It is not, even be a mere vision in the mind of many Indians. It is a mission can all take up".

16
Indian Higher Education in the Era of Globalisation

Dr Gopal Charan Biswal
Principal, Dibakar Pattanaik Institute of Advanced Studies in Education, Berhampur (Orissa)

"Where is the wisdom which we have lost in knowledge? Where is the knowledge, which we have lost in information"? (T.S. Eliot) It indicates the degrading quality of Education. General Indian Higher Education reached the pinnacle of glory and excellence in the past. Takshyasila and Nalanda universities in India in 1500 BC and 500AD respectively attracted the scholars from abroad for its enriched system of educational and quality of scholasticity . Gone are those days. The universal ideology of ancient Indian thought' Basudheiba Kutumbakam' and Tagore's basic philosophy of 'world in one nest' and 'wealth of mind which is for all' have been reflected in the present slogan of Globalization – a phenomenon of new bond of nations for mutual benefits and reciprocation.

Because of advancement of science and technology and communication system on one hand and the world wide natural devastation and eco imbalance, unnatural disharmony, war and discontentment among nations on the other hand the world – its size and shape, structure and function has been a common experience of every human society. Man has become conscious of his role in a civilized society and so his life has become more susceptible to global change now than ever before.

Globalisation is the integration of economies and societies through cross-country, flow of information, ideas, technology, goods, services, capital, finance and people'. (Ranga raja: 2003) Joseph Stiglitz defines globalisation as removal of barriers to free trade and the closer integration of national economies through trade, investment and migration of people

The word Globalization means all the nations join their hands with each other and create a kind of socio-economic environment to do business or any commercial, cultural and educational activities in which every participant nation should be benefited.

The process of globalization has transformed world trade, communications, educational activities and economic relations in the latter part of the 20th century in having a profound effect on education at the start of the 21st century.

GENESIS OF THE CONCEPT OF GLOBALISATION

Following the trade restrictions imposed by a large number of countries during 1930s and 1940s the leading nations thought of setting up a liberal World Trade System. Consequently on International Conference on Trade and Employment took place in Havana in 1947-48. Twenty three countries signed a common agreement called GATT (General Agreement on Trade and Tarrif) which came into force since Ist Jan 1948. The membership grew from 23 in 1948 to 118 in 1994 and on Jan 1995 GATT was replaced by World Trade Organisation (WTO).

GATS was one of the agreements signed under the purview of WTO which came into force from 1996. The objective of GATS is to establish multilateral framework for services similar to trade in goods. It involves the progressive liberalization of trade in 161 commercial services and specified services including education services. Commercial services include entertainment, e-commerce and Education.

According to WTO sources till July 2001, 51 countries had made commitments for education services. Out of which 42 countries had made commitments on sub sector education services.

MODES OF TRADE IN EDUCATION SERVICES:

1. Cross border supply : This is related to distance education, on line courses, internet education testing services, educational materials CDs by the member countries.

2. Consumption of service abroad : Education of foreign students among the member countries on payment of fees.

3. Commercial presence of Service : Establishing campuses, institutions in foreign countries and providing degrees, diplomas to the students of member countries.

4. Movement of natural Persons : Movement of teachers, Educationists, Experts in one country going abroad for teaching.

THE EDUCATION SERVICES ARE DIVIDED INTO FIVE SUB SECTORS

1. Primary Education : Pre-school, Primary, Adult Literacy Programmes.

2. Secondary education : High School, +2 Diploma, Vocational Technical Education of handicapped students.

3. Higher Education : Conventional Education, B.A., B.Sc., B.Com. M.A., M.Sc., M.Com. etc post – Secondary Tech. & Vocational

4. Adult and Continuing Education : Literacy Programme, Correspondence.

5. Other Education service : Short-term jobs, Coaching and Training, Recreational Education etc.

THE POSITION AND TREND OF HIGHER EDUCATION IN INDIA

Indian higher education system in the past was glorious and magnificent. The universities like Takshashila (Now in Pakisthan), Nalanda, Vikramsila were the prominent institutions of learning during the 1500 B.C. and 4th and 5th century A.D. respectively.

The system of imparting education, the subjects content disciplines and the tradition of teacher and pupil relationships were ideal and very much well commensurate with age-old Indian Philosophy, Science, Culture and traditional values and ethos of this holy land which is unique in the universe.

The modern system of university education started in India with the opening of Calcutta University, Bombay University and Madras University in 1875 which were more or less patterned in British style. There were 20 (twenty) university and 591 colleges in the country in 1947. The number of university and colleges rose to 250 and 8,529 respectively in 2002 and the number of universities and colleges rose to 356 and 15,000respectively in 2005.

HIGHER EDUCATION IN INDIA: THE PRESENT SCENE

There are nearly 356 universities, 18,000 colleges and approximately 106 lakh students and more than 4 lakh teachers.. In spite of an eye catching quantitative proliferation, India lags behind the developed countries in terms of percentage of higher education enrolment. The enrolment ratio in higher education in Canada is 100%, in USA 80%, in France 50% and in UK 30%. Where as India has only 13% enrolment in Higher Education (2003) which is less than the world average i.e 23%. Out of the total enrolment, 46% in Arts, 19.9% in Science, 17.8% in Commerce and Management. 1.3% in Education 6.9% in Engg, 3.1% in Medicine, 0.6% in Agriculture, 0.2% in Vet. Science, 3.2% in Law and 0.9% in other faculties.

The expenditure on education has gone up from 0.64% in 1951-56 to 4.11 % of GDP in 2002 –07. The goals of 6% allocation to education remains a pipe dream.

Comparing the percent of GNP spent on education, India's position is precarious. The neighbouring countries like Srilanka, China and other developed countries invest more on higher education. India has not spent 6.4% on education as suggested by Kothari Education Commission in 1964-66. At present the Govt . is spending only 2.8% of GNP on higher education.

During the last 50 years or so, higher education in India was welfare and development oriented. But it would be difficult for the academics to generate funds through higher education.

The consequences of GATS on Education is Privatization of Education and Trading with higher education. Again privatization has led to the expansion of technical education and vocational education. The present state of university education has led to low turnout of scientists, historians, journalists, philosophers and poets.

POSITIVE ASPECTS OF GLOBALISATION FOR HIGHER EDUCATION IN INDIA

1. India ranked 141 out of 173 countries in the overall education index in the year 2000. In the human development index in 2001 India ranked 127 out of 175 countries with China securing 104th and Vietnam securing 109th position. India's position in enrolment in higher education is very low in comparison to the developed countries.

   With privatization of education, the opportunities of higher education increases.
2. Kothari Education Commission and other countries emphasized on Industry — University collaboration and interaction for quality development in higher education. The private institutions sponsored by the industrial houses can more efficiently realize the industry institute interaction.
3. Resource crunch for R & D. activities may be over come by the industry sponsored institutes.
4. Private sectors are more disciplined and efficient than the govt. sectors.
5. Corporate culture will prevail in the private institutes that are absent in public institutes.
6. Due to financial problems many students of

middle class families of developing countries could not study at the reputed institutes of developed countries but because of GATS these students can pursue higher studies in the branch institutes of the developed countries established in their locality.

NEGATIVE ASPECTS OF GLOBALIZATION FOR HIGHER EDUCATION IN INDIA

1. The theories of investment by private sector is governed by the motive of profit/ return in education. Thus it becomes dangerous and counter productive in education.
2. Private institutions in India provide courses of highly technical and professional nature. IT, Computer Science, Electronics that cater to the market demands. It does not provide scope for Engineering and basic scientific study like Math, Physics, Philosophy, History, Chemistry, Mechanical, Electrical, Civil Engg. It creates imbalance in academics and thus creates a skewed development at the cost of integrated wholesome balanced development.
3. Privatization will discourage meritocracy in the sense that poor but meritorious students will not benefit from the system where as rich but low meritorious students will benefit from this privatization system.
4. Privatization does not guarantee high quality education for high cost payment.
5. International trading with Higher education creates unidirectional international relationship. It is not based on reciprocation of friendship. Developed countries reap more benefit compared to developing countries.

6. Higher education must have relevance to local needs, local culture and national ethos and values must be reflected in higher education. But with influence of GATS the developing countries including India is supposed to identify of its own. The element of unity in the diversified multi cultural society will be devoid of its image identity and glory with the amalgamation of foreign cultural elements.
7. Artificial arrangement by which foreign education tends to occupy all the space of our national mind, thus hampers the creation of a new thought power.
8. The social appeal, the cultural traditions will be neglected and rejected with the influence of GATTS.
9. The intellectual prosperity, the cultural heritage, the national values and beliefs will receive a jolt.
10. The sovereignty of our nation will be at stake or meaningless entity.
11. The provision of reduced budget on higher education as envisioned by GATS will reduce the international competitiveness of our nation and thus will make this country ever dependent on developed nations.

SUGGESTIONS TO COPE WITH THE GLOBAL CONTEXT

- Restrictions should be there on proliferation of substandard universities.
- Special Agricultural Zones instead of Special Economic Zone (SEZ) suiting to geo physical conditions and marketability.
- Advanced scales of pay for the professionals.

- Culture, Values and Indian Ethos must be reflected in higher education curriculum.
- Research and innovation on ancient Indian scriptures Vedas, Purana and cultural traditions, sages and saints must be pursued with sincere effort.
- Infrastructural facilities comparable with that of the standard institutes of foreign countries need to be weight and valued before starting higher education institutions.
- Industry, locality, university and Agriculture – Complex. linkage should be established and co-operation and collaboration must be initiated for making higher education qualitative and competitive
- Provision of reciprocal sharing between developed and developing countries on equal footings need to be made on trading of higher education.
- Eliminating research restriction on foreign scholars.
- Education should serve the community first.
- Planning, preparing, carrying out higher education need to be based on unique Indian model society to the cultural heritage, national goals and psyche and sociological thoughts.

17
Role of Education in the Era of Globalisation

Smt. Saroj Nalini Lenka
Sr. Lecturer in Education,
Nabakrushna Choudhury,
CTE, Angul. (Orissa)

INTRODUCTION

Education has always been recognized, through with varying degrees of conviction, as a vital element for individual self-fulfillment and the development of society.In the present 21st century when there is globaliation of education it has innumerable roles to shape the destiny of the future generation as well as the economic development of a country.. But it suffers from many impediments. So there is urgent need to take effective measures to eliminate these impediments to reap the benefits of education in the era of globalization.

VITAL ROLES OF EDUCATION

The idea of globalisation of education is gaining ground that it is one of the most powerful tools with which the destiny of future generation can be shaped by taking advantage of constructive trends and trying to avoid pitfalls for following reasons.

The first one is the capacity of education systems to become the key factor in development by performing a three fold function – economic, scientific and cultural.

The second one is the ability of education systems to adapt to new trends in society. This brings us to one of the fundamental responsibilities of education – i.e. to prepare for change despite the growing insecurity that fills us with doubts and uncertainties.

The third one is that of the relations between the education system and the state.

The fourth one is the promulgation of the values of openness to others and mutual understanding. The increasing interdependence of people and nations is the hallmark of 21st century, which provides scope for unprecedented international co-operation, dominated by globalisation. The society of 21st century demands.

(i) Co-operation between nations and individuals to ensure development;

(ii) Inter-cultural interaction without any tension;

(iii) Respect and tolerance for others;

(iv) High senses of responsibility amongst individuals groups and society for the world.

These should be the core values and a basis for individual group and social behaviour. They can be developed through formal and informal education. Education is one of the principal means available to foster deeper and more harmonious form of human development and thereby to reduce poverty, exclusion, ignorance, oppression and war. This century dominated by globalisation also means that education will have to adapt itself to considerable economic, social and cultural changes resulting in inevitable tensions between tradition and modernity, competition and equality of opportunity, spiritual aspirations and material reality, local interests and global considerations the unlimited expansion of knowledge and the limited capacity of human beings to assimilate it. In this context " Learning through out life" will play a key role in meeting the challenges of 21st century.

Building on the four pillars, as suggested by Delor, will constitute the foundation of education, learning to be, learning to know, learning to do and learning to live together – all societies to move towards a necessary utopia in which none of the talents hidden like buried treasure in every person are left untapped. More flexible education systems based on a new out look and a fresh approach to the learning process, are required where the value of each individual is enhanced.

It has been well recognized that economic development depends largely on the level of education and training of workforce. In this 21st century with increased global migration and global trading, education must be globalised to facilitate optimum communication and contribution of people to global economy.

Internalization of education involves, in part, true exchange of personnel and technologies among countries.

IMPEDIMENTS

The true exchange of information, education may have been impeded by barriers such as level of literacy, unequal shares of resources among countries including technology, communication facilities and current differences in the organization of education system.

SUGGESTIONS

To prepare individuals and societies for the global economy of this country, education must erase the barriers preventing true exchange of experience/ information. To achieve this purpose, education should

- Increase the level of literacy of world population so that all people can read, understand and use their own language.
- Expose students to other cultures, values to promote cross cultural understanding and tolerance of cultural differences. This must be done by requiring that part of educational programme be completed in another country.
- Forster the formation of international guidelines/ standards for various occupation and educational milestones to facilitate reorganization of educational qualifications and working experience of people who have moved from their place of origin to contribute to other countries.
- Foster research linkage and collaboration among interdisciplinary terms of various regions of the world.
- Emphasize on lifelong continuing education to prepare workers for rapid changes in knowledge and technologies.
- Promote critical thinking and adaptability to facilitate adaptation to a quick changing society.
- Formulate international language for technologies.

CONCLUSION

Education, the marvellous tool, was ever created in the mind of man. It is exclusively of the people and for the people. To get maximum benefit out of it depends on how effectively it has been constructed with reference to the purposes expected to be served by it and how well it is implemented or used. Change is the law of nature. No one can stop it. Education should be adopted ever to meet all roots of challenges for realization of the dreams of mankind with the motto. “Not to deteriorate but to develop.

18

End of Geography in Indian Higher Education

Dr Jayanti Satrusallya

Sr. Lecturer in Education,
Naba Krushna Choudhury,
College of Teacher Education,
Angul –759122 (Orissa)

The revolutionary changes occurred in rural and urban India is solely responsible for the development of technological knowledge and globalisation. More technology oriented and socially relevant system of education is highly essential to meet the challenges of 21st century. But the allocation of funds in Indian budget is inadequate to meet all these needs. Hence private public partnership and collaboration of foreign agencies are the ultimate necessity.

If we compare the Indian expenditure on higher education with other countries like: Canada, China, Brazil and Malaysia, our expenditure comes as lowest as Rs. 18,600/- in place of Rs. 5,40,000 of Malaysia. There is urgent need to increase expenditure on higher education. How to meet the deficit? Perhaps globalisation is the right answer to it. We can not keep ourselves away from the trend of technological development just on the plea that we do lack adequate funding. Our hope to establish a developed India by 2020 will not bear any fruit unless we shall sit and walk along with, after global efforts. India is rich in ideas. Only we need appropriate opportunities to materialize the ideas. Development of existing infrastructure and providing efficient teachers are equally important. Talented students are going abroad to obtain valuable degrees which can fulfill the requirements of MNCs or getting high salaried jobs. It is not a small thing that approximately 3,00,000 Indians are working in Silicon Valley. The number is quite less in India, for opportunities in India are much less in comparison to US.

Indian higher education is comprised of 350 universities and university level institutions, 18,800 colleges, 1,04,81,042 students and over 4,71,931 teachers (2005-06). Such a vast system covers general, technical and management categories of education. There is need to increase public expenditure in the field. 21st century has recognized knowledge as capital for development. Development means progress of general and technical knowledge to fulfill the need of global enterprises.

Higher Education has certain objectives like supply of skilled manpower to meet the latest requirement; to search for finding out new technology, new theory, new knowledge to update knowledge, in other words should have quest for excellence. It should have contribution to national development and should be able to foster global competencies among students. There is ultimate need to harmonise the students with the global standards. Higher educational survey establishes a fact that only four Indian higher educational institutions are included in top-level 500 global institutions. It is more than right time to think whether we should go for globalization.

The explosion of scientific and technological knowledge has made the world a global village. Nobody is prepared to consider the activities of Universities within border. Human resource has been considered as a global asset. Globalisation has become a compulsory affair for Indian Higher Education (IHE) when it became a member of GATT. Indian Higher Education has two major aims regarding quality and funding. Quality always depends on competitiveness of the product. IHE has to compete with other countries and establish itself globally. Second thing is that, it requires adequate funding for implementation of its qualitative programmes. The allocation of budget in First Five Year Plan in Higher Education was 7.2% of the total outlay, whereas it has now come down to 2.9% in the Tenth Five year Plan. Hence It is sure that IHE has to adopt new policies for resource mobilization to meet its global competitive need. From the above fact, we can conclude that globalisation is a must for Indian Higher Education.

The term "Globalisation" is further connected with various terms like WTO (World Trade Organisation), World Bank, GATS (General Agreement on Trade in Services), GATT (General Agreement on Trade and Tariff), LPG (Liberalisation, Privatisation and Globalisation). These terms and their implication has become a compulsory item in Indian Higher Education.

Article –17 of GATS Policy reflects on the item, "National Treatment" which means that Government of India and other constitutional authorities are under obligation or duty bound to provide equal and same treatment to Indian as well as foreign institutions of education. Differential and discriminatory treatment to foreign educational institutions in comparison to domestic educational institutions will be unfair and against GATS, GATT. GATS recommendations have made global economy integrated. Indian Higher Education is preparing itself to show its competencies in the field.

Due to India's membership of World Trade Organisation (WTO), General Agreement on Trade in Services (GATS) the education sector has been entered as a tradable item. Hence loss and profit must be calculated. Again due to LPG (Liberalisation, Privatisation and Globalisation) there will be disinvestments of Government share from Universities and Colleges , Multi National Companies (MNCs) and Foreign Direct Investments (FDI) will start investing in higher education sector which will lead to complete privatization. There will be more export and import (Exam) in higher education and continuous changes in higher education sector in tune with WTO, World Bank and International Monetary Fund.

Shyam Pitroda, the Chairman of Knowledge Commission has given favourable comment on entry of Private and Foreign Universities into Indian soil, so that it would be helpful in enhancing the quality of education.

Globalisation of economy has increased the responsibility of higher education. Higher education in India has to add or enhance international education. In the GATs guidelines educational services are classified into five categories like: Primary Education Services, Secondary Education Services, Higher Education Services, Adult and Continuing Education Services and other Education Services which includes special training programmes conducted by industries and organized coaching classes. Keeping in view the above categories we can enter into the four reorganized modes of trade in education defined by GATs.

(i) **Cross border supply:** Where educational services are supplied across national boundaries, from one country to another in the form of printed materials or on line education via Internet.

(ii) **Consumption Abroad:** Which means movement of consumers (students) from one country to another. Normally students going abroad for regular study or research fall in this category.

(iii) **Commercial Presence:** It means presence of a foreign education service provider in a host country and conducting various programmes through establishment of institutions.

(iv) **Movement of Natural Persons:** The pressure of a foreign teachers in host country to provide service is the last category of service.

Our esteemed former President of India Dr. APJ Abdul Kalam has visioned India in the way of igniting Indian youth. It has been estimated that Indian Youth will exceed 50% of the total population by 2020. For obtaining sustained National Development at least 20% of the total population in the age group of 18-24 should get benefit of higher education. Globalisation alone can fulfill the expectation.

There is a fear that small and developing states can not compete with globalisation. Recent summit on 23rd September, 2007 where Honourable Vice President India Dr. Hameed Ansari presided over a function and an opinion came up as "Globalisation is the danger to the Indian Higher Education". Where our whole nation has one slogan "Garibi Hatao", globalisation has no position in the country.

In this case this much can be argued that, one time considered as a poor country, China could recover from its poverty within 15 years through inclusion of foreign scientific and technological knowledge. There is no doubt that quality education provided by reputed international providers will be accessible only to the privileged few who can pay for it. Globalisation will favour the persons who have capacity and willingess to pay the higher fees. But we, should not also foreget the quality higher education in India is going very smoothly and getting international reputation. Examples are not rare. The Common Admission Test (CAT) of Indian Institute of Management, the Joint Entrance Examination (JEE) of the Indian Institute of Technology, the National Eligibility TEST (NET) of the University Grants Commission and the Council of Scientific and Industrial Research (CSIR), the Graduate Aptitude Test in Engineering (GATE), the Pre-Medical Test (PMT) and the Pre-Engineering Test (PET) and some of the examples which can be applied in Foreign soil. IHE has to interact and compete with others to enhance its quality. Hence IHE sector should be developed in such a way to accommodate the global need. Education in India is regarded as a welfare item and not a profit-making item. Some private entrepreneurs have made it profit making and set a trend for higher expenses. It is our responsibility to create atmosphere for sustained national development and hence we can not close the entry of globalisation as discussed under four points earlier (cross border supply, consumption abroad, commercial presence and movement of natural persons).

When whole world has been considered as a global village, it needs unity, uniformity and integration of education and its system. Multi National companies (MNCs) are considering Indian employment market as cheaper and hence they do prefer to recruit Indians in their offices at lower salaries. They need to modify the Indian Education System which would fit to their requirement. It is a regular trend to send Indian job holders under MNCs abroad and get them adopted to their corporate system through education and training. It will be highly beneficial to the job seekers at MNCs if they would be able to get those kind of education in Indian soil through entry of foreign educational institutes in India. The Indian students would not need to go abroad with higher expenses for undergoing Faculty, Exchange Programme. This particular programme can be implemented in India with tie up of various industries and offices inside India. In the emerging global employment market studies like IT, ICT can provide key to job seekers.

We the residents of Orissa are not unfamiliar with the names like POSCO, MITTAL, VEDANT, STARELITE etc. We have got direct experiences regarding globalisation though not in the field of higher education. Indian democracy is quite fit to face all types of global situations. India has already made available as much as 15% of seats in its higher educational institutions including technical ones to foreign students.

INSTITUTIONS ENGAGED FOR PROMOTION OF GLOBALISATION OF HIGHER EDUCATION IN INDIA

The Ministry of Human Resource Development has set up Educational Consultants India Limited (EDCIL) as a nodal agency for promotion of higher education abroad and placement of foreign students in Indian institutions.

The Govt. of India has launched a scheme named

DASA (District Administration of Students Abroad) which monitors 15% seats in premier technical institutions in India.

The University Grants Commission has identified various disciplines for export purpose. Those are Business Management and Entrepreneurship, Engineering and Technology, Computer Science, Health Science etc. UGC has launched this programme for Promotion of Indian Higher Education Abroad (PIHEAD)

CONCLUSION

In the above context we can conclude that we shall have to prepare a positive climate for globalisation of Indian Higher Education. We are not at the cross road rather we are already on the road of globalisation.

A position paper prepared by the Association of Indian Universities on "General Agreement on Trade in Services and its Implications on Higher Education" on 21st November, 2004 gives a negative comment on globalisation with the statement. "It will not be desirable for the country to liberalise Indian Higher Education system under GATs " (University News – 43 (06), Fe. 07-13,2005. Despite the resolution, we cannot keep ourselves away from GATS or globalisation due to various reasons listed below:

- Inclusion of education in GATS under World Trade Origanisation's provision has encouraged for globalisation of education.
- Faster development of IT has made globalisation easier as education could be disseminated through various modes.
- Higher demand for professionals in diverse fields has led the students to go abroad.

- More job creation through globalisation of higher education.
- Higher Income Generation is another cause for globalisation of education.
- Students having good financial capability want to gain experience of diverse world and diverse work place.
- Developing countries have less infrastructure of higher education in comparison to developed countries and it is another cause for globalisation.
- Liberal economic policies of Banks in granting loans for higher education purpose is another cause leading to globalisation of IHE.
- Globalisation helps in creating global network for education and research.

Hence, let the globalisation of Indian Higher Education work smoothly.

REFERENCES

1. - *Internationalisation of Indian Higher Education*, University News, Association of Indian Universities, 16 Comrade Indrajit Gupta Marg (Kotla Marg), New Delhi –110002, Vol – 39, No.15.
2. – *GATS and its implications on Higher Education*, AIU Position paper. Ibid, Vol. 43, No.6.
3. Pandey , V.C. (2005); *Education and Globalisation.*
4. Joshi, K.M. (2001); *Higher Education: Issues and options*, Ed OZA.

19

Globalization and Challenges to Higher Education in India

Dr. Jyostna Sahoo
Sr. Lecturer in Education,
Radhanath Institute of Advanced
Studies in Education,
Cuttack –753002 (Orissa)

INTRODUCTION

Globalization means integration of economies and societies through cross country flow of information, ideas, technology, goods, services, capital, finance, and the people. In other words it refers to removal of barriers to free trade and the close integration of national economy – "a world in one nest". The coming century dominated by globalization will bring with it enduring tensions to overcome, tensions between global and local, the universal and individual, tradition and modernity, long term and short term considerations, competition and equity of opportunity, the unlimited expansion of knowledge and the limited capacity of human beings to assimilate it and the spiritual and the material whatever the diversity of culture, the systems of social organization, there is a universal challenge of reinventing the democratic ideal to create or maintain social cohesion.

GATS (2006) AND EDUCATION

The General agreement on Trade in Services (GATS) is an agreement between countries who are signatories to World Trade Organization (WTO). Education is one of the Services covered under GATS, as marketing of "Education" is now-a-days a more profitable proposition with very great potentials and possibilities. It is included in 12 classified sectors covered in 161 services. Free unfettered trade in education seems to be eminent. The educational systems of all the countries of the world are to be opened up as per GATS mandate. Therefore education must posses in built quality and saleable skills competing with others with the best of the world needs to be nurtured.

WTO classification list W/120) divided educational Services into five parts i.e.;

a) Primary Education Services.

b) Secondary Education Services.

c) Higher Education Services.

d) Adult Education

e) Other Education Services (Professional, Technical etc.)

In a globally competitive world, India will be loser in the international educational trade market, if quality and relevance are not be built, empowerment and status of the teachers do not enhance, suitable infrastructural facilities are not be available, obsolete curriculum and courses are not properly substituted and revamped. In a globally competitive world, it is quality of education that can survive and sustain a nation.

CHALLENGES - THE CONCEPTUAL PARADIGM:

In the coming decades, there will be a shift from teaching society to a knowledge society advancing towards a learning society and ultimately to a society of wisdom. The major focus will be on transition "from learning to be, to learning to become." It may be mentioned that we have already crossed the three waves – Agrarian, Industrial and Information (Alvin, Toffler). Coming millennium will be marked by a generation of fourth wave having profiles like spiritualization and a responsive society with increasing aspects of globalisation, accountability, information technology and assimilation of power of knowledge (GAIA) (Maynard and Mehrtens). Education of the future will be based on four pillars "Learning to know, learning to do, learning to live together and learning to be".

CHALLENGES TO HIGHER EDUCATION

At present (as per 2006 report) there are 342 universities including 18 central universities. Out of them 211 universities are State Universities. 95 Deemed Universities, 5 Institutions under State Act, 13 Institutions of National Importance, 40 Agriculture Universities providing allied subjects, 25 in Medicine, 49 Engineering and Technology, 18 Legal Universities, 11 Open Universities, 7 Information and Technology and 6 Women Universities. At present there are approximately 17000 Colleges, 4.5 lakh teachers and 99.54 lakh students.

COMMITTEES AND COMMISSIONS

The post independence period had marked with

different committees and commissions for development of Higher Education.

1. University Education Commission 1948-49.
2. Report of the Education Commission 1964-66.
3. National Policy on Education – 1968.
4. National Commission for Teachers –1983.
5. Challenges of Education. A Policy perspective – 1985.
6. National Policy on Education 1986 & 1992 and their programme of actions.
7. Towards an Enlightened and Human Societies 1990.
8. Towards new Educational Management UGC, 1990.
9. Learning the Treasure within – UNESCO International Commission on Education for twenty first Century, 1996.
10. Indian Knowledge Commission Report – 2006.

REGULATING AND QUALITY CONTROL STATUTORY BODY OF HIGHER EDUCATION

University Grants Commission (UGC) is the regulating body for quality management of higher education, now concentrating on setting up of autonomous colleges, redesigning courses, and revamping examination system, creation of Council of Higher Education in the State, developing alternative models of University management, conducting national qualifying examination for the recruitment of teachers (NET), imparting. Training and Orientation to teachers through special grants to Academic Staff Colleges and University Departments and empowerment of teachers through workshops and Seminars.

National Accreditation and Assessment Council (NAAC) is an autonomous council under UGC to carry out periodical assessment of universities and colleges in the country. Besides there are All India Council of Technical Education (AICTE), National Council of Teacher Education (NCTE), Indian Council of Agriculture Research (ICAR), Medical Council of India (MCI), Nursing Council, Pharmacy Council, Indian Council of Medical Research (ICMR), Bar Council of India, Distance Education Council (DEC), Institute of Chartered Accountancy India (ICAI). All these are statutory bodies. As per the recommendation of NPE (1986) State Council of Higher Education have been set up at state level for state level planning co-ordination and feed back to UGC.

RECOMMENDATION OF NATIONAL KNOWLEDGE COMMISSION

1. Right to Higher Education : For Access, Retention, and Success, there is need for creation of more universities (1500 and 50 National universities) for the country along with more institutions of Higher Education (General Professional, Technical and Vocational as per manpower need and to meet the demand of the youth).

- Instead of multiplicity of regulating system, there must be one independent apex body with branches Independent Regulating Authority for Higher Education (IRAHE) may be created.
- Increase of public spending on Education – 6% of GDP in Education and 1.5% on Higher Education.
- 20% of expenditure shall be met by fees, needy students shall be provided with fees waiver plus scholarship and UGC is to supplement Grants to

public institutions in Higher Education.

2. Excellence : University must be the sub centre of research and innovation, Revision of Curricular activities in every three years, Introduction of continuous internal assessment and credit system, synergy between teaching and research, strengthening resource allocation and infrastructural facilities along with better working conditions to attract and retain talented faculty member must be ensured. Emphasis will be led on quality and excellence.

3. Structural Reforms : Structural Reforms of the Universities to enhance accountability, autonomy and social audit, must be taken up. Emphasis on up-gradation of knowledge, incentives for performance and empowerment of teachers must be ensured, appointment of Vice-Chancellor on search process and peer judgement free from direct or indirect intervention of the government, may be introduced. University courts, Academic Council, Executive Council, may be restructured to accelerate progress and not to act as stumbling block. Creation of smaller Universities with a view to make it easier to manage and responsive to change is required. .

4. Restructuring under graduate Colleges : More Autonomous Colleges, developments of cluster colleges with autonomy, remodeling of general colleges as community colleges with vocational education and formal education, creation of a Central Board and also State Board for under graduate education with the power of affiliation, provision of quality bench marks, examination and development of need based courses are some of the recommendations.

5. Promotion of Enhanced Quality : Provision of accountability to society and creation of accountability within, stringent information discloser and transparency in examination and evaluation, evaluation of courses and teachers by students and peer groups, enhancement of ICT, infrastructure, website, web service, e-education and e-library facility, creation of a knowledge net work connecting all universities and colleges for on line open resource, creation of facilities for communication technology and teleconferencing, development of appropriate means to attract and retain talented faculty members, formulation of appropriate policy for entry of foreign universities in the country and Indian universities abroad ensure a level. Field for foreign and domestic institutions within the country will help to enhance quality; diversity and pluralism in higher education should be introduced to avoid one size, fits all approaches.

6. Ensure access to Deserving Students : Creation of more opportunities so that good students should not be denied for admission into higher education due to financial constraints. Well-funded national scholarship scheme targeting economically under privileged students may be created for economically and socially disadvantaged groups.

The coming century dominated by globalization will gear towards world-class education based on value. Knowledge gaps will be bridged through net working of institutions, growth of educational complexes and wider access to e-learning and continuing education.

VISION AND TASK AHEAD

A University stands for humanism, for tolerance, for reason, for the adventure of ideas and for the search of truth. It stands for the onward march of the human race towards higher objective. Universities are places of ideals and idealism. If the Universities discharge their duties adequately then learning endeavour in each educational institution will be to spot talents, kindle the spark within and empower each student to strive for excellence. Therefore the management structure of universities should be on the principle of self-governance based on participation, decentralization, autonomy and accountability. A large measures of autonomy is being stimulated in the system to encourage freedom to select staff and students, determine curriculum and degree standards and to allocate funds.

In this age of a techno-scientific revolution, when the sheer quantity of knowledge and information is expanding exponentially, when the needs of a constantly growing and increasing varied students are burgeoning, the quality training for teachers and the quality of teaching in higher institutions demand top priority. As we move towards a learning society, even human activity will require contributions from experts and this will place the entire section of higher education in sharp focus. The major focus will be – "All teachers should teach and students should study with the professional motto, "Quality teaching with quality education blended with research and innovation."

Education in the coming days will be based on eight major dimensions – Soul, Soil, Society, Skills, Science And Technology, Solidarity, Service and Survivals. The ultimate objectives will be to achieve Life Enrichment Education (L.E.E), Life Skills Education (L.S.E.) and Life Value Education (L.V.E)

In brief higher education should be diversified so as to take into account their functions and duties as centres of knowledge, as the hub centre of research, as places of professional training as the cross roads for learning through out life and as partners in international co-operation.

REFERENCES

1. Government of India, (1986) & (1992); *National Policy on Education 1986 with modification under taken 1992* Ministry of HRD, Department of Education, New Delhi.
2. Govt. of India (1992); *Programme of Action 1992* Ministry of Human Resource Development, Department of Education.
3. UNESCO (1996); *Learning the Treasurer within Report of International Commission on Education for the Twenty First Century.*
4. UNESCO (1998); *Report of the World Conference on Higher Education. Higher Education in the Twenty First Century, Vision and Action.*
5. Raya, R. Prabhakar, (2001), *TQM for Higher Education,* Journal for All India Association for Educational Research (Vol-13, 2nd March).
6. NAAC (2005); *Institutional Accreditation Manual for Self-appraisal of Teacher Education.*
7. Sen, S. (2005) *Towards Global Culture in Higher Education Institutions in India,* NAAC News, July 2005.
8. National Knowledge Commission, New Delhi, (2006): *Note on Higher Education.*
9. Darial, John Sri, (2006); *Higher Education, Teacher Education, and Distance Education: What is Quality and who says so?* NAAC, News April.

20

Challenges of Globalization and Higher Education in India

Smt. Babilata Shroff
Lecturer in Economics, D.A.V. College,
Titilagarh, Dist. Bolangir, Orissa

EDUCATION DURING PRE-INDEPENDENCE PERIOD

India had a glorious past in terms of academics. During ancient times, Indian educational Centres and Universities were the temples of human knowledge. Students used to study at Taxsila, Patiliputra and Ujjaini. The popular subjects included Science, Medicine, Spiritualism, Astrology, Philosophy, Politics, Economics, etc. Even students from abroad used to study in these reputed institutions of learning. There were exchanges of students' knowledge and books. Indian educational system was respected around the world for its high quality syllabi and learned teachers. But foreign invasions and disturbances scratched our educational system and polity.

CHANGING TRENDS IN EDUCATION AFTER INDEPENDENCE

After Independence the existing syllabi were found theoretical in nature. Teaching methods were primitive. We followed Lord McCaulay's system of Education which tried to produce clerks. Realizing this, our education policy changed the system of education which can promote national progress, develop a sense of common citizenship and build national integration. Emphasis and attention was on science, technology and moral values. Acquisition, correlation, transmission and further enhancement of natural sciences, social sciences and technology were considered to be the basic function of education.

EDUCATION, BUSINESS AND INDUSTRY

During 1960s it was realized that despite our various educational policies declared from time to time, our educational system was not linked to Indian industry and business. This lack of continuity between the two major engines of growth has proved to be harmful for our national, industrial and economic growth..

Realising this in 1966 the Kothari Commission Report on education emphasizing manpower planning approach and later Sam Pitroda's Knowledge Commission Report presented in Jan 12, 2007 suggesting reforms taking into account the economic and social forces operating in the country were announced.

GLOBALIZATION AND NEW CHALLENGES

Globalization has opened the domestic economy to the world market offering challenges and opportunities. While facing the trend of globalization, (i.e. interaction of the country relating to production, trading and financial transactions with the industrialized developed countries.) the developing countries like India having a large domestic market, broad-based industrial and infrastructural sectors, abundant supply of cheap labour, a huge number of educated and trained manpower and adequate natural resources to attain competitiveness, India needs from its producers higher rate of productiveness, improved quality products and innovations in products and process technology.

In order to attain International competitiveness companies will have to enter into strategic alliances and collaboration in order to bring in state of the art technology to reduce cost, improve efficiency and penetrate and capture global markets with joint efforts.

It is certainly an opportunity and challenge for the Indian industries ensuring second generation reforms, growing trend of mergers and acquisition of financial inclusion, technology initiatives and need to evolve adequate safety regulations for their operations.

Entry of foreign players as well as new domestic players on the one hand and pleasing today's demanding customers on the other; innovative and sincere efforts have become essential for the organizations to make themselves stronger and stronger, if they have to survive and thrive. The organizations active, in enriching their strength have been found establishing an edge and compelling the weaker ones to say either good bye or restructure and revamp their units with the changing business environment.

A more professional approach is needed to manage their business.

GLOBALIZATION AND GROWTH OF MNCS

Followed by globalization there is growth of MNCs or TNCs. MNCs (Mainly dominated by American countries) are exercising a huge control on the business of the world economy. They are diversifying their products in various countries (mainly in India and China) and can sell easily whatever product they manufacture. The MNCs are growing faster due to;

i) Their international image (world wide reputation)

ii) Marketing superiorities arising out of its up-to-date market information system, reputation, effective advertisement, sales promotion technique and warehousing facility.

iii) Financial superiority over the national firms.

iv) Technological superiorities

v) Effective product innovations due to their superior research and development facilities.

vi) In an UDC like India, people have craze for the products of MNCs instead of their indigenous products, this tendency has helped the MNCs to expand the market of their products in India.

GLOBALISATION, GROWTH OF MNCS AND MANPOWER REQUIREMENT

Now the technology of the advanced countries is far superior to ours. While employing manpower these MNCs are searching for brains (talents having capturing capacity) and provide them training to get adjusted with the nature of the job. They expect from them (i) smart use of money (ii) colourful investment, asset allocation taking into account risk appetite (Rebalancing and or reviewing the portfolio at least once a year); (iii) Snapshot of the cash flow and (iv) high return and risk management with tax efficient investment option. They are the job providers to those who can work in multiple skills, technologies, domains and platforms. If found inefficient he/she will be removed from the job, if found suitable and capable handsome packages are provided. Now-a-days out sourcing companies are widely seen. Here the job holders have to be more challenging as failure or inefficiency reduces the reputation of the employee as well as the out sourcing companies (the employer). Now a days when we look into the career/job section of the newspapers and magazines we find jobs like Engineer, Manager/Technical Manger, Specialist, Manger/ Reader, Finance and Account Manager, Team Leader, Finance Manager, Finance Executive Accounts Manager, Relationship Manager, Bus, Development Consultant, Senior Consultant, Territory Manager, Lead Generation Manager, Lead Software Solutions, Bus. Development/Accounting Manager, Market Research Analyst, Marketing Communication Specialist, Estate Maintenance Manager, Senior Designer piping, Technical Architect Java, Network Programming, Protocol Developer, Subject Matter Expert (revenue, cost margin capex, etc.) Strategic Planning Bus. Analyst, Head Corporate Communication etc.

In the most of these jobs I could not find the mention of essential qualification. But knowledge of computer is essential.

Previously job advertisements were like B.E. – Civil/ Mechanical/ Electrical etc., MBA – Finance/ Marketing, C.A. , etc.

To achieve international competitiveness the domestic players as well as the public sector enterprises are also searching for innovative ways by employing skilled manpower.

GLOBALISATION AND CHANGING TRENDS IN EDUCATION

As we approach the 21st Century, it is becoming increasingly clear that the ability to cope with rapid changes in the higher education system will become the primary measure of sources at both micro and macro levels. Change is occurring faster every day. Many societies have shifted from "Industrial era to "Information" era. A few years back it was felt that the volume of information that becomes available doubles every 4 to 5 years. But now it is felt that it changes each 2 years. Day by day the requirements rise.

Stating it is another way, total of all human knowledge that was available to an under graduate in 1997 will be less than 1% of that in 2050 (Gandhe, 2002)

These changes have a major impact on education and training. In fact, education and training are undergoing a major change. Some are:

i. From Institution based learning to far learning education with just in-time knowledge provision.
ii. From fixed curricula to personalized curricula.
iii. From front-ended education to life -long education.
iv. From teaching to learning.

There is a want for knowing the distance between what is needed to be done and what is?

USE OF COMMUNICATION AND INFORMATION TECHNOLOGIES

Advances in Communication and Information Technologies are at the heart of these changes. Speaking on education of the future, Buckminster Fuller said that "Education is going to be number one amongst the great world industries, within which will flourish an educational machine technology that will provide tools such as the individually selected and articulated two–way TV and an inter continentally networked documentary call up system operative on any home two way set."

These developments are quite effective for higher education and also in the process of learning by providing the learner freedom to choose what, where and when to learn and from which source.

Convergence between Information and Communication Technologies has resulted in considerably enhanced capacity to transfer data, voice and vision, at an enormous speed and has become an important aspect in higher education. For learning process to become more effective and conducive to higher education, some developments in communications and information technologies are needed. These are:

i. Integration of television, tele-communication, and computers, through digitization and compression techniques.

ii. Reduced costs and more flexible user applications of tele-communications through developments such as ISDN (Integrated Service Design Network)/Fiber Optics (Study of cable networking from exchanges to home)/Cellular Radios (Ex. FM- Frequency Modulus).

iii. Miniaturization (tiny cameras, microphones, small high resolution display screens).

iv. Increased processing power, through new micro chip development and advanced software techniques, and

v. More powerful and user friendly commands and

software tools, making it much easier for users to create and communicate their own materials.

EMERGING TECHNOLOGY AND LEARNING PROCESS

One of the most important features of Emerging Technologies is their improved capacity to facilitate learning. Information comes to us with uncanny speeds and ways never before imagined. It can be downright overwhelming.

With development and growth of middle classes there is an increasing demand for job-oriented courses. Traditionally, we were of the view that " Want to be a Doctor – go for +2 Science with Bi. P.C, Engineer – go for +2 Science with P.C.M., I.A.S./O.A.S./Banking/ other competitive exams – go for +2, +3 and then Post Graduation either in Arts or Science, C.A. / I.C.W.A/ C.S. and after sometime M.B.A. Demand for computer technicians, also MCA or go for commerce education. After the generation of computers and demand for computer technicians do MCA or BCA – go for B.Sc. with Maths. Or +2 Science respectively. So on".

But now the system has changed. Except a few lines (MBBS, etc.) all other courses are open. There is no-entry bar. For any job whether related to investment, advertisement, marketing, financing, public relation, project evaluation, data processing or accounting or sum of any of these two or three; institutions- especially private institutions absorb any degree holder. In interviews and entrance they chalk out the student's capacity to deal with the tool, cope, adjust and capture the training given according to the requirement. Here the question of specialization comes from training and learning. Deviations are found from the traditional undergraduate and advanced courses.

Ex. – B.Sc. /B.E. /B.A. /B.Com. – M.B.A.

B.A. /B.Sc. /B.Com. /B.E. /M.B.A. – M.C.A.

B.E. /B.A. /B.Sc. /B.Com. /M.B.A /C.A. – M.C.A. /Networking (CCNA) /CDAC /Insurance Management /etc.

B.Sc. /B.Com. /B.E. /M.B.A. /B.A. – For ex. B.E. /M.B.A. /B.Sc. - Actuarial Science.

With widening of job market after globalization and tremendous developments in the field of science and technology, education technology has not remained far behind. Emergence of Information Technology including the satellite-based telecommunication system has generated potential of a sea-change in the education system not only all over India, but all over the World.

Education, now, is not something to be completed before entering the job market; but it has become a life-long occupation. Place of work will be the place of education. The paces with which these changes will take place depend upon the pace with which Information Technology will be put into operation to the cause of education.

Information Highway*, Teletex** and Videotex*** are the new information-age services that has become widespread among home and business users.

* **Information Highway :** High speed data networks used to transport information and link people who want to be connected with others.

** **Teletex :** One-way service in which pages of information from a central data base are broadcast on regular television signals.

*** **Videotex :** More sophisticated two way service using telephone lines.

E-mail, Tele-conferencing (audio-video) and Computer conferencing are common activities on the Internet and other electronic networks. With the Information Highways becoming a reality in many developed countries, Conferencing Technology has come to be used in a large way in collaborative distance and open learning.

Some learning tasks are also involved such as attentiveness, idea generation, concept elaboration, feedback, etc. which could be fulfilled through distance education.

In this era of modern technologies in education, it is pre-supposed that the learners have access to a wide range of high specification information and communication technologies that these technologies can be used at times in circumstances that are convenient for learners and optimal for effective study; and the learners have sufficient familiarity or experience of using them.

Internet leads to an increasingly 'free market' in education, protecting the user from national, state or provincial boundaries. In the era of increased demand for high specification information and communication technology, the job-seeker must have the access and talent for the specialized course. Here the under graduate level syllabi will be helpful, if the basics are known before hand.

GLOBALISATION & MUSHROOMING OF PRIVATE EDUCATIONAL INSTITUTIONS

With economic progress on the one hand and the growing middle class & their rising aspirations on the other, demand for higher education continued to rise. Most of the parents are willing to spend on the higher education of their children as they see it as the best form of investment for their upward mobility (Agrawal, 2007). Over the past 60 years, while the population increased three fold, higher education enrolment grew more than 100 times. Initially due to limited access of seats in the Govt. educational institutions matching with growing demand; private educational institutions were started. But later, they gained popularity either due to their quality or advertising skills or low performance of the ward (which could be fulfilled by monetary compensation) or some other attractions like possibility of placement, scope of still higher studies, etc. During 1980s they started growing but during 1990s got momentum. Now in almost all professional courses about 80% enrollment is in private institutions.

The fee structure of the private educational institutions is higher than the public institutions. While the basic objective of higher education is to meet the need of qualified people in the economy by acquiring skill & competencies for productive activities in the economy & create new knowledge; with the growth of private sector, higher education has become commercialized.

FUTURE PROSPECTS

As per the Kothari Commission, education at all stages should foster transformation & strengthen democratic ideals. There should be a well planned strategy for higher education to face the challenges of post globalization changes.

Estimation should be made on human resource requirement at each level. A collective effort by the teachers, students, educationists, educational institutions, policy makers & the policy implementing agencies is essential to streamline the education system so that skills, knowledge, employability & enterprise evolve for the benefit of the country.

For the students : To face the challenges of the time and become more competent and efficient the students must develop sense of attentiveness, effective idea generation, concept elaboration, capacity to acquire, etc. A few thousand students passing out from the IITs and IIMs will not take India to great heights. Currently only 9% to10 % of students passing out from colleges are skilled enough to get effective employment. They should be prepared to accept the challenges of globalization & open their brains to the learning sources.

There is a need to drastically restructure the university set up, curriculum & the examination system.

Effective (Timely & adequately) restructuring of syllabus : To serve the cause of young India the academic world should come in tune with reality. Manpower requirements at each level should be estimated & specialized syllabi should be prescribed for each stream. While interviewing 50 executives, officers and others like managers, analysts, leaders, etc. from various MNCs, private sector organizations and public sector undertakings, all agreed a fundamental knowledge in all or at least some of the subjects like skill of communication, use of computer technology, financial management, marketing management, operation management, budgeting, accounting, investment, insurance, project planning, merger and acquisition etc. during under graduate level with practical knowledge also (whether they are from engineering, business or computer background) for those who want to join that sector. Thus a need based restructuring of syllabus should be made. Practical knowledge from practical fields should be given in place of examples and solutions from books at the under graduate level.

For the teachers : There is a need for skill up gradation for teachers who are the engines of these future job seekers. They should be reoriented each two or three years to satisfy the changing need of the time, so that the students will be the survivors of this information explosion effectively and turn knowledgeable. They have to be expert in helping learners navigate through this sea of information rather than pretending to be effective transformers of that information into knowledge.

Outsourcing: Wherever deficiency and incapability among existing teachers is found, experts from reputed and relevant institution having specialization in that particular field should be taken to help the students and maintain continuity in teaching as per requirement.

Now a day's private players are more active in this respect.

For private educational institutions : An unregulated private higher education may have serious repercussions on quality & cost. Hence they should be regulated effectively, so that cost reduction will take place along with improvement in quality. There should be a fair quality competition.

Assistance to colleges\universities : 'Quiet crises in higher education should be wiped out by providing assistance to the colleges\universities who are not able to meet academic & infrastructural requirements. Again in institutions with high concentration of SC, ST & economically backward students, provision should be made on enhancing support. There is also need for a decentralized management with adequate attention & representation of parents (most of the private institutions do it in practice).

Industry and Education interface : Education should be planned keeping in view the requirements of industry & business. Similarly industry must supply relevant inputs like money, training, equipment, employment security, etc. So that the educational system will remain tuned to the needs of the industry.

Higher education in India seems to be a sick child. As compared to the developed countries we are bellow standard. Currently 3.5% of India's GDP is on education, which has somewhat "divorced" education from the reality. *This should be enhanced.* A *higher education roadmap* should be prepared. A *holistic approach* is required.

In a changing world, future shape of things is unpredictable; so there is a need for an education policy which contains a build in flexibility to adjust to the changing circumstances.

Globalization & higher education in rural India : Even in this age of science & technology 72% of our brethren live in rural India & a majority of them study in kerosene lanterns & candles. Even a large mass do not get two meals of food everyday. Their first struggle is for existence & then comes the question of education & then higher education.

Are they in a position to reap the benefits of Information & Communication Technology or at best computers? All of them are not going to join the MNCs. Thus the mass of population who are supposed to join the primary sector should be trained & skilled accordingly. There is a need for taking development to their doorsteps by bringing 'appropriate education technology' i.e. 'location specific education' for water harvesting, agricultural waste management, organic farming, crop diversification, crop rotation, cottage industries, upgradation in animal rearing, education on health, nutrition, sewing for girls, etc., which could help sustaining their own livelihood. Gradually they may be stepped up to the lessons related to Biotechnology, Genetics, use of Information & Communication Technology, weather forecasting, etc. Facing the challenges of globalization this will be the best higher education for them. This will need workshops, laboratories, etc. as well as specially trained teachers. Here the policy makers are assumed to work as catalysts for their speedy upliftment & an instrument for poverty alleviation.

As the aim of higher education is 'life enhancing' the policy measures related to higher education should assume the role of a force multiplier to accelerate the pace of development.

Partnership and financial contribution of centre, state and private educational managements are also inevitable.

There should be LOCAL ACTION with a GLOBAL VISION.

CONCLUSION

All the Industries (including education) are on the upward sloping learning curve with regard to imbibing and inculcating new and latest technological version. Once Karan Paul, Chairman, Apeejay Surendra Group told "Globalization has changed the business environment, people need to work harder, longer and there is more pressure to perform."

Really Globalization demands from the people to work in multiple skills, technologies, domain and platforms". Addressing National Conference of Vice-Chancellors in Delhi the HRD Minister Mr. Arjun Singh said, "India is not knocking at the doors of the World, but the World is knocking at the doors of India. It is up to us to open the door or keep it shut."

REFERENCES

1. *MNCs to dominate technology hiring wave in India.* Jobs-career- technology.
2. *Taxmen to Monitor MNCs,* the Times of India.
3. *Outsourcing practices of Major Technology MNCs in India.*
4. *Top ten BPO companies in India.*
5. *Opportunities for MNCs in India: North East.*
6. Gandhe, S.K.; *Distance Education: New Technologies in the 21st Century.*
7. Shroff, B.; *Emerging Trends in Service Sector Marketing in India during the Post Globalization Era.*
8. *Education for Personality Development;* Competition Success Review, Jan. 2005.
9. *National Employment Guarantee: A pipe dream?* ; Competition Success Review, Jan. 2005.
10. Krishna Murthi, G.K.V.Raju and Ila Patel; *"Corporate Action in Community Development: Evolution, Imperatives and issues."*
11. *"Adult Education in the Context of Economic Restructuring".* A paper presented at the Irma- C11 Workshop on Corporate Action in Community Development.
12. Mishra, Ratnakar; *E-Business, a lifestyle.*
13. Nanda, R.K.; *Capital Market of Information Technology and its Influence.*
14. Dutt, Rudra; *New Economic Policy and its Impact on Industrial Relations and Employment in India.*
15. Singh, Man Mohan; *New Economic Policy and Challenges before the Labour Economists.*
16. Krishna Murthi, J.; *The Load Stars in Education.*
17. *Asian Vision with Global Perspective;* India Today, 17th Sept. 2007 issue.

18. *Nurturing the Industry Specialist Professionals*, India Today, 17th Sept. 2007 issue.
19. Mishra, Alok K (2006).; *Strategies for Inclusive Growth: Learning from Global Experience;* The Indian Banker; Dec. Vol.1-No.12.
20. Kumar, P. Suresh (2006); *Outsourcing in the Banking Sector-An Analysis*; The Indian Banker, April, Vol.1-No.4.
21. Bakshi, D.C. (2006); *Knowledge Commission & Rural India*, Yojana, July.
22. Kumar, Shashi Bhushan (2005); Education in India: Flushed with Highest Literacy Jump; Chronicle, Feb.
23. *Teacher Education: Draft Curriculum Framework for Quality Education*; Chronicle, Dec.2005.
24. ILO(2006); *Globalization Failing to Create New Jobs*; Chronicle; Feb.
25. Sundaram, K(2006); On Backwardness & Fair Access to Higher Education; EPW; Dec. 16,

21

The Challenges of Higher Education and Tips to Turn them into Opportunities

Dr. Tilottama Senapati
Assistant Director, Directorate of T.E. & S.C.E.R.T., Orissa, Bhubaneswar.

INTRODUCTION

With the introduction of economic reform in Indian Economy in 1991, and replacement of GATT (General Agreement on Trade and Tariff) by WTO (World Trade Organisation) at international level (1995) and signing of General Agreement on Trade in Services (1996); 12 classified sectors including Education, covering 161 services have become tradable commodity, being controlled by market forces i.e. demand and supply. As a consequence of which the situation in the field of education especially Higher Education has been changed and new trends emerged. The emerged trends have posed many challenges. So at this context, it is pertinent to find out the challenges in the field of Higher Education and to suggest suitable tips to turn them into opportunities.

OBJECTIVES

Considering the threats of Higher Education the study was planned with the following objectives.

- To find out the new challenges of Higher Education.
- To suggest suitable tips to turn them into opportunities.

METHODOLOGY

The study was prepared collecting data from secondary sources. Many journals, research findings have been referred for the above purpose.

THE NEW CHALLENGES OF HIGHER EDUCATION

In the present context Higher Education faces many challenges.

i) The Education system has acquired a dualistic character because of the finance provided by government is inadequate. 75% of our children go through an educational programme of poor, even rock bottom, quality provided by colleges and universities while 25% benefit from a small number of quality educational institutions.

ii) Political interference especially in universities and colleges forced teachers and student unions to interfere with the normal functioning of the institutions. These phenomena are bound to cause administrative, operational and financial problems. As a result the govt. policies and programmes are not effectively implemented and the reforms introduced within the educational system are slow.

iii) Syllabi of many universities reveal academic backwardness. They spell out subjects which are neither job oriented nor life oriented.

iv) The real ills of the present educational system are its elitist nature, its heavy push out and drop out rate, its scandalously poor environment growing unemployed and unemployable product outcome, indifference to the illiterates, minimal learning and evaluation system and widening gap between the overt curriculum and the hidden curriculum.

v) Academic and administrative problems faced by our educational institutions are further compounded by govt. control.

vi) Quantitative expansion is taking place being unmindful of quality assurance system.

vii) Globalization of education is going to pose serious threats before the conventional system of higher education in India. In the international knowledge market our universities have to compete with the foreign players.

viii) When there will be developments in electronic educational technology and international mobility of students, assessment and monitoring of learning apart from the instructional process poses problems.

ix) All universities are struggling to find funds as the state funding is shrinking to alarmingly low levels. The fiscal constraints, coupled with increasing demand, has led to overcrowding, deteriorating infrastructure, lack of resources for non-salary expenditures such as text books, laboratory equipment etc. New programmes often did not have the resources necessary to ensure minimum quality standards. The poor compensation made difficult to recruit and retain qualified personnel. Due to cut down of capital investment by Universities as a consequence of decreasing financial resources from govt., learning and research materials and equipment deteriorated. Many of the state universities are facing difficulty even in the payment of the salary bills of its employees including teachers.

x) a) In traditional curricula a huge gap between the demand and supply of higher education exists due to the increase in the need of education by the masses and the lack of resources to provide required infrastructure to fulfill this need. At present only eight percent of the eligible age group of Indians is enrolled in Higher Education in our Universities and institutions leaving a large proportion of the eligible population to the open learning / distance education system and unscrupulous foreign players with dubious credentials.

b) Quality higher education to-day is in demand by all the stakeholders in education as the students, guardians, employers and society. But due to lack of resources higher education institutions in developing countries often find themselves unable to provide and sustain good quality of education, thus leaving the field open to resource rich transnational players – to enter the educational market of developing nations. The increase in demand for quality education leads to influx of talent from the country to the developed world. In either case whether through international student mobility or through commercial presence, it is the resource starved institutions of the developing world which stand to lose both financially and talented manpower benefits the rich nation at the cost of the poor.

c) The traditional curricula provided by higher education institutions in India unable to keep up with the changing demands of the job market, has lost out on the relevance front.

xi. Commercialization of education will result in withdrawal of subsidy by the government and will raise the cost of education. This situation will have serious implications for the equity objectives set forth in the constitution. The enhancement of cost of education will be transferred on to the students and will result in admitting students according to paying capacity rather than merit. The long term consequence of blocking entry in to the deserving will affect the country's development and consequential economic prosperity too.

xii. In view of GATS prescribing the principle of non-discrimination, the Indian Universities are to be treated at par with foreign providers of education. The Foreign Service providers will either compete with Indian Universities for government subsidy or make a case for withdrawal of subsidy. Either way it is the native institutions which will stand to lose both (a) by withdrawal of subsidy (b) by subjecting them to market forces for which they are ill equipped. The withdrawal of subsidy will further impoverish the already resource starved native institutions forcing them to enhance costs, there by reducing access to the meritorious poor.

xiii. The domestic institutions and universities will lose out on the competition with foreign education providers because of the low fees charged and consequent poor infrastructure and resources. Fundamental knowledge, which is invaluable will lose out in competition to knowledge having immediate market value.

xiv. In India the National Assessment and Accreditation Council (NAAC) accredits institutions of general education and National Board of Accreditation (NBA) accredits technical institutions. However the national system of accreditation may not solve the issues in transnational education for the following reasons.

a) International credibility of national accreditation can not be guaranteed.

b) National and International accreditation may provide different decisions about the same degree.

c) National Accreditation body may not be able to desist the pressure of global brand name providers trying to enter the market.

d) Our programmes and degrees accredited by our national system may not receive equivalence to credits aboard. Thus leading to competitive disadvantage to our institutions.

xv. When private initiative is keen on promoting professional value, there will be hardly any takers for social sciences like history, philosophy, fine arts, literature, archaeology or anthropology. The neglect of social sciences will further remove from the horizon of our minds the grim reminders of our social condition. The students will focus on problem solving rather than critical thinking.

xvi. Profit motive is the ultimate aim of the investment of private sectors. But it is dangerous and counter productive in education sectors.

xvii. Due to GATS adoption of the international trade with higher education all benefits will go to the developed nations. For example in Dhaka city of Bangladesh there are 42 centres of foreign universities but there is no such centre of any Bangladesh university in foreign country.

TIPS TO MEET THE CHALLENGES OF HIGHER EDUCATION

In the present globalization steps have already been taken to meet the emerged challenges of higher education but its fruit is yet to be tested. So some tips are suggested to meet the new challenges of higher education.

i. The government of the country and the state should take measures to check the dualistic characters of the educational institutions. The financially poor institutions should chalk out policy measures for improving their status.

ii. Unnecessary political interference should be curtailed to let the institutions to run smoothly in their administrative and financial spheres.

iii. Syllabus of the universities should be updated and job oriented courses are to be introduced.

iv. Drop out rate in educational institutions should be checked by developing a special package for them and minimizing the gap between overt and hidden curriculum.

v. In the name of government, excessive interference is undesirable.

vi. For quality assurance courses should be related to life.

vii. We require to provide international level courses in Social Science, Humanities, Applied Arts and Foreign Languages in order to attract a greater number of foreign students and bring in the much needed financial resources in the form of fees and having expenses contributed by foreign students to our economy.

viii. International students of America origin opt for short term courses, hence to gain from transnational education India must develop internationally relevant short term courses in Social Sciences, Humanities, Applied Arts and other areas in which we possess expertise such as Yoga, Vedic Mathematics, Alternative Systems of Medicine etc.

ix. It is necessary to work with higher education institutions to develop effective ways to assess learning accomplishment not time spent in a certain place or with a certain programme. They also will need to develop inspection methods appropriate to a new focus on learning regardless of its setting or provider.

x. It is necessary to assess the educational needs of the developed world and also understand our own strength, locate the areas of education in which we have expertise such as Alternate system of Medicine, Yoga, Traditional wisdom and culture etc. and develop courses of international standards in order to attract international students and the much needed financial resources. Thus transnational education will not merely be a drain on our economy but rather it will contribute positively to our Indian economy.

To compensate for decreasing financial resources from the federal government universities have to cut down on capital investment.

xi) Improvement in the educational infrastructure of domestic educational institutions must take a priority. The fee structure needs to be rationalized. Physical infrastructure like class rooms, libraries, hostels, and sports facilities should be of international standards.

xii) Quality education needs to be developed in India in order to stress the brain drain as well as prevent economic losses. Improvement of quality of education imported is required so as to make it comparable to international standards, failing which this very survival will be in danger.

xiii) The Global Alliance of Transnational Education (GATE), an international organization envisioned by the corporate sector and founded in 1995 by Jones International Limited is the answer to this problem of quality. The principles of GATE is to assist institutions and organizations in the development and evaluation of quality education that crosses borders.

xiv) Besides the above, the customer satisfaction is the key for upgrading quality as without full customer satisfaction it is not possible to increase market share. The customers of education are students. Student satisfaction should be used as an effective instrument for raising the quality programmes of study.

xv) There should be provision of scholarships for poor and meritorious students otherwise due to the increase in cost of education the students who have not capacity to afford will be deprived of the facilities.

xvi) A mutual recognition of degrees and credits can be the only basis of the Transnational Education. Therefore, a mutually acceptable accreditation process needs to be evolved.

xvii) The private institutes are to stay till government is in position to adequate investment in higher education sectors, but with government controls and monitoring so that quality is maintained and any sort of undesirable imbalance is prevented.

xviii) For permitting foreign universities to operate the monitoring of course curriculum with national ethics and philosophy and condition for equal opportunities at their countries be imposed only not to make the trade unidirectional as in software business.

CONCLUSION

In the changing global scenario the higher education poses many challenges. Although various suggestions have been prescribed to turn them into opportunities how far they will be effective is yet to visualize. The market players in the field of higher education are not expected to have any socio-cultural vision. They see globalize knowledge as tradable commodity, once they are successful in converting Indian "Gurukul' in to their super-bazar, the students will have became an attractive euphemism for customer. Then ruthless market forces will play freely in our vital field of higher – education. The market players of giant globalization may gobble up our glorious culture and traditions. Though they will sponsor for our intellectual growth may limit our terrain. We should care to spare our thought and resist the temptation to fall in to the trap of privatization of education before it is too late. When fees formed less than 14% of the total expenditure in Britain and Higher education is primarily a state responsibility in USA and govt. support directly to 78% of total enrolments in public institutions and indirectly to 22% of total enrollment in private institutions, how can Govt. of India, constitutionally committed to equity and social justice subject higher education to the logic of the market forces ?

REFERENCES

1. Arasu J.G. Valan (2003*); Impact of Globalisation and WTO on Higher Education in India,* University News, Association of Indian Universities, AIU House, 16 Comrade Indrajit Gupta Marg (Kotla Marg) New Delhi – 110002, August-08-14, Vol.43, No.32, PP-17-22.
2. Ahmed Samsuddin (2005); *Globalisation and Higher Education in India,* University News, Association of Indian Universities, AIU House, 16 Comrade Indrajit Gupta Marg (Kotla Marg) New Delhi – 110002, August-22-28, Vol.43, No.32, PP-12-13.
3. Bhattacharya BB & Bhumia(2005); *Threats and Opportunities in Higher Education in the context of GATS,* University News, Association of Indian Universities, AIU House, 16 Comrade Indrajit Gupta Marg (Kotla Marg) New Delhi – 110002, Oct 31-Nov 06, Vol.43m No.44, Pp-15-16.
4. Jalal A (2005); *Emerging Trends in Education in the Global Era,* Kurukshetra, Director Publication Division, Ministry of I&B, Govt. of India, Patiala House, New Delhi-110001, July, Vol-53, No.8, pp.18-19.
5. Joseph Thomas (2006); *Higher Education in the changing Global Scenario,* University News, Association of Indian Universities, AIU House, 16 Comrade Indrajit Gupta Marg (Kotla Marg) New Delhi – 110002, April-03-09, Vol.44, No.14, pp.1-5.
6. Khanna Pratibha (2005); *Transnational Education : Issues and Implications,* University News, Association of Indian Universities, AIU House, 16 Comrade Indrajit Gupta Marg (Kotla Marg) New Delhi – 110002, August-08-14, Vol.43, No.32, pp.9-16.

7. Singh Raminder (2005); *Privatization of Higher Education in the Era of Globalisation,* University News, Association of Indian Universities, AIU House, 16 Comrade Indrajit Gupta Marg (Kotla Marg) New Delhi – 110002, August-08-14, Vol.43, No.34, PP-9-11.

22

Globalisation of Higher Education : Its Emerging Trends and Challenges

Dr. Rajan Kumar Sahoo
Reader in Economics,
U.N.S Mahavidyalaya, Khairabad,
Mugpal, Jajpur-755009 (ORISSA)

INTRODUCTION

The New Economic Policy was introduced in India in 1991 in which liberalisation, privatization and globalization are three principal processes for economic upliftment. While liberalization means to liberate the economy from the control imposed by the government, privatization means giving more scope to the private sector abolishing licensing system. On the other hand globalization is a process of integration of the national economy with the world economy as a result of which national market will be linked with international market and the restrictions on imports and exports will be progressively abolished. Globalisation of education refers to the operation of educational services on a world wide scale. It is the concept of internationalization which refers to the co-operation between nations in order to develop standards of educational services acceptable to all. This process gained momentum when GATT (General Agreement on Trade and Tariff) was replaced by WTO (World Trade Organisation) in 1995 and its signing of GATS (General Agreement on Trade in Services) in 1996. So in the changing scenario, there emerged new trends and many challenges. So in this context there is every necessity to have a probe into these trends and challenges

OBJECTIVES

Considering the importance of higher education in the present context the study was planned with the following objectives :

- To study the emerging trends in Higher Education.
- To find out the new challenges which arise out of the emerging trends of Higher Education.

METHODOLOGY

The study was prepared collecting data from secondary sources. Many books, journals research reports have been consulted for the above purpose.

THE EMERGING TRENDS IN HIGHER EDUCATION

In the changing situation the following trends have been developed in higher education.

MODES OF PROVIDING TRANSNATIONAL HIGHER EDUCATION

The signing of GATS (General Agreement on Trade in Services) by WTO member countries has made education a tradable commodity. GATS has resulted in education being included in 12 classified sectors covering 161 services for which a legal frame work has been drawn occurs through four distinct modes of supply.

1. Cross-border Supply : Crossing national barriers, education is provided through distant mode in which the learner is geographically separated from the provider.

2. Inter-Institutional Arrangements : When two or more countries undertake joint study programmes having mutual recognition and credit transfers .

3. Consumption Abroad : The education of foreign students in institutions of the host country. This is the most common form of trade in education from the developing world to the developed countries. This transnational student mobility benefits the developed world more than nations like India, which is the top most supplier.

4. Commercial presence : Institutions from another country may grant franchise or establish campuses in the host country to offer their programmes or qualifications to students stationed in the host country itself. The host country grants recognition to such courses offered. Commercial presence of foreign players in the educational sector is the most threatening to the developing countries because its resource starved institutions fall out of the competition and secondly it promotes privatization thus enhancing the cost and restricting access and equity.

GLOBAL AND CULTURAL UNIFICATION

Through efficient modes of communication there is a process of global and cultural unification revolution in the scientific and technological fields and cybernetics and electronic information transmission are sweeping the world. The globalization of economy has led to internationalization of higher education, not merely for economic benefits, but also for increased social interaction and promotion of international understandings.

VIEW OF HIGHER EDUCATION AS COMMERCIAL PRODUCT

Now higher education is viewed as a commercial product that can be bought and sold at the market place. The universities which were viewed as custodians of knowledge, would have to function like business concerns looking for buyers of their product in order to increase their profits. The corporate houses regard education as an industry where the students are consumers, teachers are service producers and the institutions or companies catering to education services are organizer and the teaching, learning process is no longer for the building of a nation but a business for profit making.

ACQUIRE OF ENGLISH LANGUAGE A STATUS OF LINGUA FRANCA

The process of globalization has given English Language a status of lingua franca of international communication as it has made dissemination of information easier and quicker. Such a situation will place the product of private English Medium Schools at an advantageous position as compared to others.

WIDE USE OF EDUCATIONAL TECHNOLOGY

The wide use of educational technology in higher education has expanded access and spawned new ways of teaching and learning. Use of electronics educational technology creates an increased number of institutions to offer distance learning and with much higher number of students enrolled.

MOBILIZATION OF STUDENTS INTERNATIONALLY

Development of electronic educational technology will cause international student mobility.

SOCIAL & PRIVATE RETURNS OF HIGHER EDUCATION & PRIMARY EDUCATION

According to UNESCO and World Bank report social and private returns of higher education are less than those of primary and secondary education. It is estimated that social return of primary education is 25% while that of higher education is only one percent. So the returns of higher education are largely personal therefore the government of India started reducing the share of allocation for higher education.

INCREASE IN PRIVATE PROVISIONS

As increasing expansion of higher education will not be attached by proportional rise in public expenditure, there may happen an increase in private provisions or self-financing institutions. The Ambani-Birla report rightly stated, a private Universities Bill should be legislated to encourage the establishment of new private universities, a redefinition of Government role in higher education would call for a major privatization of university education system in India.

EMPLOYMENT OPPORTUNITIES & PRIVATE SECTOR

Majority of employment opportunities are in private sector and this sector is very choosy. The sector employs only those who possess skills and competencies required by it.

RELATIONSHIP BETWEEN STUDENTS & TEACHERS

The students active participation in the process of learning on their own initiative will remove the one-sided authoritarian teacher-student relationship. The teachers authority will now be based on his ability and creativity to contribute and help students to learn on their own. The other driving force for raising quality will be the commitment of teacher to their students and to the pursuit of excellence.

INCREASE OF OPPORTUNITIES FOR PRIVATE STUDIES AND ENROLLMENT

With private participation the opportunities of higher studies increases and this may increase the enrolment figure.

INSTITUTES SPONSORED BY INDUSTRY HOUSES CAN BE MORE EFFICIENT

The private institutes sponsored by the industry houses can more efficiently and meaningfully realize the industry institute interaction for fruitful achievement.

PRIVATE INSTITUTE MORE DISCIPLINED

Private sector are more disciplined and efficient than the government sectors.

SCOPE FOR THE STUDENTS OF DEVELOPING COUNTRIES STUDY AT THE UNIVERSITIES OF THE DEVELOPED COUNTRIES

Due to financial crunch, the students of the developing countries could not study at the universities of the developed countries. But due to GATS Universities of the developed countries are opening branches at the developing countries that will provide a scope to the students of the developing countries to study at the universities of the developed countries at a relatively low cost.

NEW CHALLENGES OF HIGHER EDUCATION

In the field of higher education there is all round deterioration is quality education, world class faculty are not attracted and retained in our system. Our institutions are starving for funds, for development, our universities are functioning as mere examination conducting bodies, our curriculum is unsuited to meet the job demands, dominance of caste system in recruitment, Rampant corruption in all walks of life. Rich students pay but poor students pray for education, existing access to teaching learning is affected in the absence of adequate safeguards, under / partial utilization of infrastructure and manpower, incapability of Govt. to fulfill the constitutional obligation of equity and social justice, and unmanageable socio-cultural problems.

SUGGESTIONS

So there should be industry institution interaction / encouragement of foreign collaboration, Exchange of faculty of students, development of joint courses, international exchange of scholars, universal acceptance of certificate or credits for wider marketability, fund raising measures, measures for quality enhancement, introduction of job oriented courses, elimination of caste based recruitment, checking of leakages, provision of scholarships for poor meritorious students, adequate safeguards, development & full utilization opportunity of infrastructure & manpower and commitment of the Govt. can convert the challenges of higher education into opportunities.

CONCLUSION

We have to wake up from the deep slumber and discard the old, rusted and outdated skills. We must replace the feudal, traditional higher learning and adopt a new more dynamic educational approach that is a must for survival and growth. This is a possibility only when all the concerned – Professors, teachers, students and leaders of our nation must answer affirmatively.

REFERENCES

1. Arasu J.G. Valan (2003); *Impact of Globalisation and WTO on Higher Education in India,* University News, Association of Indian Universities, AIU House, 16 Comrade Indrajit Gupta Marg (Kotla Marg) New Delhi – 110002, August-08-14, Vol.43, No.32, PP-17-22.
2. Ahmed Samsuddin (2005); *Globalisation and Higher Education in India,* University News, Association of Indian Universities, AIU House, 16 Comrade Indrajit Gupta Marg (Kotla Marg) New Delhi – 110002, August-22-28, Vol.43, No.32, PP-12-13.
3. Bhattacharya BB & Bhumia(2005); *Threats and Opportunities in Higher Education in the context of GATS* University News, Association of Indian Universities, AIU House, 16 Comrade Indrajit Gupta Marg (Kotla Marg) New Delhi – 110002, Oct 31-Nov 06, Vol. 43, No.44, Pp-15-16.
4. Jalal A (2005); *Emerging Trends in Education in the Global Era,* Kurukshetra, Director Publication Division, Ministry of I&B, Govt. of India, Patiala House, New Delhi-110001, July, Vol-53, No.8, pp.18-19.
5. Joseph Thomas (2006); *Higher Education in he changing Global Scenario,* University News, University News, Association of Indian Universities, AIU House, 16 Comrade Indrajit Gupta Marg (Kotla Marg) New Delhi – 110002, April-03-09, Vol.44, No.14, pp.1-5.
6. Khanna Pratibha (2005); *Transnational Education : Issues and Implications,* University News, Association of Indian Universities, AIU House, 16 Comrade Indrajit Gupta Marg (Kotla Marg) New Delhi – 110002, August-08-14, Vol.43, No.32, pp.9-16.

7. Singh Raminder (2005); *Privatization of Higher Education in the Era of Globalisation* , University News, Association of Indian Universities, AIU House, 16 Comrade Indrajit Gupta Marg (Kotla Marg) New Delhi – 110002, August-08-14, Vol.43, No.34, PP-9-11